Birds of Prey

Birds of Prey

IN THE
AMERICAN
WEST

photographs by

**TOM
VEZO**

text by

**RICHARD L.
GLINSKI**

**RIO NUEVO
PUBLISHERS**
TUCSON, ARIZONA

Rio Nuevo Publishers
An imprint of Treasure Chest Books
P.O. Box 5250, Tucson, AZ 85703-0250
(520) 623-9558

editor: Ronald J. Foreman

design: Larry Lindahl,
    Lindahl–Bryant Studio, Sedona, AZ

Text and Introduction
  © 2002 Richard L. Glinski

Photographs and "Photographing Birds of Prey"
  © 2002 Tom Vezo

Printed in Korea

10 9 8 7 6 5 4 3 2 1

Cover: *bald eagle*

Back cover: *ferruginous pygmy-owl*

Half title page: *barn owl wing feathers*

Title page spread: *(left) male American
kestrel, (top right) rufous morph red-tailed
hawk, (bottom right) burrowing owl*

Facing page: *prairie falcon*

Dedication page: *bald eagle*

Introduction (page 1): *Richard L. Glinski
photo by Tom Vezo*

"Photographing Birds of Prey" (page 3):
Tom Vezo photo by W. Ross Humphreys

Note: The northern harrier (p. 30), northern goshawk (p.39), prairie falcon (pp. iv-v and 86-89), barn
owl (p. 91), northern pygmy owl (p. 99), and Mexican spotted owl (p. 110), photographed for this
book were born and/or rehabilitated in captivity. All other bird species shown were photographed as
I found them, in the wild. —Tom Vezo

Library of Congress Cataloging-in-Publication Data

Vezo, Tom, 1946–
    Birds of prey in the American West: photographs by Tom Vezo;
    text by Richard L. Glinski.
        p. cm.
    ISBN 1-887896-38-4 (pbk.)
    1. Birds of prey—West (U.S.) 2. Birds of prey—West (U.S.)—
    Pictorial works. I. Glinski, Richard L., 1950– II. Title.
    QL677.78 .V49 2002
    598.9'0978'022—dc21   2002014536

Dedication

*For Dorothy, Alison,
Katy, and Michael—
my new found family.*

TOM VEZO

*To all the young and
budding raptor enthusiasts
in the American West.*

RICHARD L. GLINSKI

Species List
in taxonomic order

black vulture

Harris's hawk

crested caracara

burrowing owl

Introduction

RICHARD L. GLINSKI

FROM THE EASTERN SLOPES of the Rocky Mountains to the shores of the Pacific Ocean, the American West is a vast and varied land characterized by environmental extremes. This region encompasses the greatest variety of habitats in North America, ranging from torrid deserts to frigid tundra, from grassy savannas to forested mountains. Here you will discover America's Crown Jewels: the great national parks, plus scores of national and state forests, monuments, conservation areas, wildlife sanctuaries, and wilderness areas.

Soaring over this majestic landscape is an equally impressive array of birds of prey. In fact, the American West is home to the greatest variety of birds of prey on the continent. These birds range in size from the five-inch-tall elf owl to the mighty California condor, with its nearly ten-foot-wide wingspan.

Birds of prey comprise a distinguished group in the avian world that includes eagles, hawks, falcons, and owls. Collectively, these flesh-eating birds are known as raptors. Residing at the top of the food chain, raptors are uniquely adapted for capturing and dismembering live prey. Vultures are flesh-eating birds that have historically been grouped with the birds of prey although, technically speaking, they are quite different. In the interest of tradition, we present them in *Birds of Prey in the American West* and describe some of the characteristics that separate them from the true raptors.

Since the dawn of recorded time, mankind has maintained a special bond with birds of prey. For example, the pharaohs of ancient Egypt ruled as the incarnation of the falcon-god Horus, supreme deity in the Egyptian pantheon. Later, eagles graced

(left) crested caracara

the standards of Imperial Roman legions. Native peoples of the American West have long revered hawks and eagles and have used the feathers of these birds as sacred talismans in spiritual ceremonies.

Unfortunately, the relationship between man and bird has had its dark side, too. Raptors have been persecuted by persons who saw them only as game and livestock killers, or who could not understand the importance of predation in the cycle of life.

For most people, modern conservation strategies to save endangered raptors have afforded them their first glimpse into the secret lives of birds of prey. Televised reports of these recovery efforts have brought the plight of raptors, and fascinating aspects of their ecology, into the living rooms of millions of people.

We have created *Birds of Prey in the American West* in that same spirit. It is meant to be an introduction and a celebration, not a field guide. We do not offer all-inclusive accounts of every species of raptor found in the American West, but we do feature thirty-four birds of prey which are most prominent or significant, including several which have been listed as endangered or threatened by the U.S. Fish and Wildlife Service. Tom Vezo's remarkable photographs capture these birds as most people may never have seen them before, and in all aspects of life.

Our purpose here is to share what we have been privileged to learn through many years of observation and hands-on experience, photographing and working with these wondrous creatures in the wild. Our hope is that this book will promote a deeper respect and admiration for these regal birds, and inspire more people to embrace and support the values of wildlife conservation.

Photographing Birds of Prey

TOM VEZO

I HAVE ALWAYS BEEN INSPIRED by the sight of a raptor, circling effortlessly in an azure sky with its wings spread wide to catch the wind. Watching these powerful birds as they soar among the clouds and rocky cathedrals, surveying the sublime landscapes of the American West, I am filled with an exhilarating sense of wonder and the freedom of flight.

When we catch a glimpse of these birds of prey in flight, we can appreciate their power, speed, and aggressiveness, but there are so many other aspects to the lives of these wild and mysterious creatures that most of us seldom see. These are the things I always look for when I set out to photograph birds of prey. These birds live in a wide range of habitats, and their hunting, mating, nesting, and feeding habits are extremely difficult to document on film. Because they are very reclusive by nature, it can be especially challenging to find them and enter their domain.

I want others to see these birds at home in their natural environment. More raptor species can be found in the American West than anywhere else in North America, and there is no more exciting backdrop for a photographer than the picturesque and infinitely varied western landscape.

Like the birds, I am most at home in the unspoiled vastness of the Wild West. From the snow-capped mountains off Alaska's Kenai Peninsula where the bald eagle soars, to Arizona's lush Sonoran Desert where the ferruginous pygmy owl nests in the giant saguaro cactus, to the wide open spaces in-between where hawks and golden eagle reside on sheer craggy cliffs: these are the special places my photo safaris have taken me.

Like any other wildlife photographer, I have had to contend with so many variables; bad weather, poor light, equipment break-downs, uncooperative subjects, and even forest fires. But when it all comes together and I return with that one special photo, it makes all the effort worthwhile. That's what I live for.

Getting to some locations was not without risk, like the time I had to climb to the top of a high, windy cliff with all my cumber-some equipment and sit in a blind at the precipice just so I could get the best angle on the nest of a golden eagle. I bushwhacked into backcountry where the undergrowth was so dense that it was impossible to see where I was stepping and I could only pray that I wouldn't get bit by a snake. I took my four-wheel-drive truck up trails and across streams where the clearance was so low that it's a wonder I never got stuck. My quests for perfect pictures often took me many miles off the main road, where my cell phone would have been useless.

I'll never forget the thrill of discovering a pair of American kestrels nesting in a giant saguaro. I set up a permanent blind and monitored it for a couple of days to make sure the adults would accept it, and then for the next several days I came to the site at dawn and waited for the birds to become active. Some mornings I would wait for hours for them to make their first food drop, and then I would only have time to take ten to fifteen frames before they took off again. That would be it for that morning because they would not feed again until the light was no longer good for photography. I would have to return the next morning and try again. Sitting and waiting for each magic moment, I would wonder what sort of prey they would bring back to the nest this time. Would it be a lizard, a snake, or something else? One morning I was amazed to see the male return with a young bird in its mouth. I was so excited that I completely blew the first couple of shots, but that final frame was the keeper.

The most difficult species for me to photograph were the owls. Almost every night for about a month, I would head out into the field at sunset and get home around midnight. One night the

(left) red-tailed hawk

elf owl I was trying to photograph landed on the flash unit of my camera, only a foot away from my head. To him, it was simply a handy perch from which to hunt insects and, although I was so close I could have reached out and touched him, my presence didn't seem to bother him. There was no way I could capture the moment on film, but the experience is nevertheless etched on my heart. I love to be out in the wilderness, enjoying all that nature has to offer, but it is these intimate encounters with wildlife that I treasure the most.

Birds of Prey in the American West offers avid birders and armchair naturalists alike the opportunity to see and appreciate these wonderful creatures as my colleague, Rich Glinski, and I have experienced them: wild and free. We also hope it can serve to raise awareness, particularly among young people who might not necessarily be very interested in our natural world. We have a duty to teach them how important these creatures are, how fragile their habitats can be, and what their generation and generations to come stand to lose if we don't protect them.

3

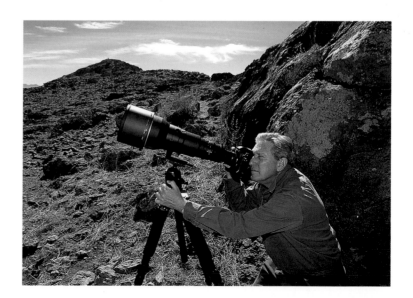

*Its distinctive flight pattern of four to
eight quick wing beats, followed by a glide,
gives this big black scavenger away.*

Black
Vulture

Coragyps atratus

AT FIRST GLANCE, you might mistake the black vulture for an eagle, as it slowly circles in the arid skies of southern Arizona, Texas, and Mexico. But its distinctive flight pattern of four to eight quick wing beats, followed by a glide, gives this big black scavenger away.

The black vulture's wingspan measures about five feet and is flat rather than dihedral, or "v" shaped, like that of the turkey vulture. Prominent white patches appear near the wingtips, and the tail is broad and short. The black vulture's long legs and toes, most evident when the bird is on the ground, also may be seen extending a little beyond the end of the short tail when the bird is in flight.

Black vultures have a poor sense of smell but remarkable vision. Thus, they tend to hunt from great heights, where they can more readily see the carcass of a dead animal as well as competing vultures that are either circling or perched on the ground. Having found its prize, a black vulture can be fairly aggressive, kicking and biting other vultures to gain position or a morsel of food.

Feeding on carrion can be messy, so the featherless, naked head of the vulture is uniquely adapted for burrowing into the

(left) White wingtips and a broad, short tail distinguish the black vulture in flight.

rotting flesh of dead animals. This adaptation also permits sunlight to reach the skin of the bird's head, keeping it dry and free of bacteria.

Black vultures appear quite content to spend much of the time on the ground, and they also are comfortable in the presence of human beings. Along some areas of coastal Mexico, black vultures may be seen walking among chickens looking for scraps of food, seemingly domesticated.

The white, crusty substance evident on the legs of the vulture is the dried residue of directly deposited excrement. Evaporation of liquid wastes from the surface of its legs produces a cooling effect. This behavior, termed urohydrosis, enables the vulture to dissipate a significant amount of body heat.

Like other vultures, this bird lays its eggs in depressions scraped on the floor of a shallow cave or on a cliff, and regurgitates food directly into the mouths of its young. Black vultures roost communally in trees, or on cliffs or rock outcrops. Since they cannot soar as efficiently as turkey vultures, they generally leave the roost later in the morning when thermal updrafts are better developed.

Black vultures spend much of their time on the ground (above and right), and the carrion on which they feed can also attract turkey vultures and crested caracaras (left).

6

Black vultures have a poor sense of smell but remarkable vision.

Unlike black vultures, turkey vultures have a keen sense of smell and locate food more by scent than by sight.

T**HE TURKEY VULTURE** is one of the most conspicuous large birds of the American West. European emigrants called this huge bird a buzzard, after a type of common hawk they had known in the Old World. In truth, carrion eaters like the turkey vulture and its genetic cousins, the black vulture and California condor, are more closely related to the stork family than to hawks and eagles.

Turkey Vulture

Cathartes aura

The flight of the turkey vulture has been celebrated in Western folklore and song for generations. Soaring effortlessly with its six-foot wingspan held in a dihedral, or "v" shape, the turkey vulture exhibits a characteristic rocking, rather than flapping, motion, which is best suited for stabilizing flight in the turbulent air of thermal updrafts.

Turkey vultures may live alone or in groups numbering more than several dozen individuals. Unlike black vultures, turkey vultures have a keen sense of smell and locate food more by scent than by sight. When they smell a dead animal, they land and watch for clues to the food's whereabouts. Thus they are able to locate small prey that other vulture species, which depend on sight alone, would miss. Turkey vultures spend most of the day in flight, and as the sun begins to set and the thermal currents wane, they

(left) With its wrinkled, red head, the adult turkey vulture bears a passing resemblance to the turkey.

The flight of the turkey vulture has been celebrated in Western folklore and song for generations.

gather in communal flocks to roost in trees or on cliffs. In the morning, they can be found with spread wings, basking in the sun, waiting for the sun to produce thermals that will once again take them aloft.

The bare head of a turkey vulture is black at birth and turns red when the bird is a little over a year old. With its wrinkled, red head and habit of walking on the ground while eating, the adult bird bears a passing resemblance to the turkey, which explains the origin of its name.

Turkey vultures breed throughout the American West. They do not build nests. Instead, the female merely scrapes a shallow depression in the debris of an elevated cave, cliff, or other such protective substrate, in which she lays one or two eggs. To feed its young, a parent vulture regurgitates the putrid contents of its crop into the gaping mouths of its nestlings.

In late September, turkey vultures from northern portions of the American West move south into Mexico, where they are particularly abundant along coastal areas. Populations in the southern portions of California, Arizona, and Texas tend to remain year round. Turkey vultures that migrate south for the winter return to the north beginning in March. The best time to observe turkey vultures is in springtime, when groups of a dozen or more begin to make the journey north. If you are lucky, at sunset, you may see them swarm around a large tree or cliff, looking for a place to roost for the night.

(right) The turkey vulture rocks its body, rather than flaps its wings, as it soars in the turbulent air of thermal updrafts.

The California condor, with a wingspan approaching ten feet, is the largest bird in North America.

PERCHED ON A ROCK HALF A BILLION YEARS OLD, this bird seems right at home. His ancestors once lived here, at the Grand Canyon of Arizona, thousands of years ago, and his homecoming was heralded with great fanfare. With a wingspan approaching ten feet, the California condor is the largest bird in North America. Until very recently, it also had the dubious distinction of being the most endangered bird of prey on the continent as well. Thus, the return of the California condor to the canyon country of Arizona was a major milestone in one of the most dramatic endangered species recovery efforts in wildlife conservation history.

California Condor

Gymnogyps californianus

The California condor evolved to feed on the carcasses of large mammals, such as mammoths and camels, which were once common in North America but became extinct here about ten thousand years ago, at the end of the Pleistocene Period. Over the last few thousand years, condors have found refuge along the coastal regions of the West, where populations of large marine mammals such as sea lions and seals are abundant.

Today, California condors face a much more insidious threat: lead poisoning. Autopsies of California condors discovered dead in the wild found fatally high traces of lead in the birds' systems. Apparently, the wild birds were scavenging the discarded remains of game animals and were ingesting bullet fragments along with the flesh.

(left) Each captive-bred California condor is fitted with a numbered wing tag and radio transmitter before it is released.

*Before final release, researchers
fit each California condor
with a numbered wing tag
and a radio transmitter.*

As the population of California condors continued to dwindle, wildlife officials initiated banding programs to track their movements. By 1983, there were only twenty-two birds left. With the species teetering on the brink of extinction, wildlife authorities captured all surviving California condors and housed them in special facilities at two zoos in California, where they could be fed only uncontaminated food.

These birds served as parental stock for an innovative captive breeding program, the objective of which is to produce as many viable young California condors as quickly as possible. Breeding pairs are forced to "double clutch," or lay two eggs annually instead of one. When the female lays the first egg, it is removed from the nest to be incubated artificially, and the hatchling is

reared using substitute puppet "parents." The female will then lay another egg to replace the missing one, and the parents are permitted to raise this hatchling.

In 1992, the first young birds reared in this manner by the California Condor Recovery Program were brought to the Sespe Condor Sanctuary in southern California. In the years since, many more have been released in California, Arizona, and Baja California, Mexico.

To help the captive-bred California condors acclimate safely to their new surroundings, biologists first put them into what are essentially large, cave-like boxes anchored to ridge-tops and fitted with mesh barriers that protect the young birds from predatory golden eagles and bears. Before final release, researchers fit each California condor with a numbered wing tag and a radio transmitter so that the bird can be quickly identified and located after the screen is removed and it is free to fly.

To ensure that inexperienced juvenile and adult California condors get enough to eat, wildlife workers will supplement their diets with uncontaminated food. These birds have huge appetites: an adult California condor can hold up to four pounds of carrion, or about twenty percent of its weight, in its crop.

Mortality among birds released is southern California is still unacceptably high, but the population in central California appears to be doing better and the "new," more remote habitat at the Grand Canyon may also prove to be hospitable in the long run. Thanks to the dedication and hard work of a multitude of individuals and organizations both public and private, California condors are once again gracing the skies of the American West.

California Condor Recovery Program personnel use antennae (left) to keep track of each bird in the wild (right).

Ospreys build large nests atop prominent features such as pine snags, rock pinnacles, and telephone poles.

AMONG BIRDS OF PREY, the osprey is in a class by itself. Not a true hawk, eagle, or falcon, the osprey is uniquely designed to capture fish. It has long legs to reach deep into the water; feet that are covered with tiny, prickly scales underneath to assist in holding slippery fish; and long, sharply curved talons to insure their grasp. Their toes are reversible: each foot can grab a fish with two toes on each side, rather than three in front and one behind like other diurnal birds of prey. Also, their nostrils can close as they dive into the water, and their feathers are compact and oily to shed water.

Osprey

Pandion haliatus

Ospreys seldom venture far from water because their diet consists almost exclusively of live fish. They hunt mainly on the wing, hovering or circling up to one hundred feet in altitude, then diving feet-first into the water—as deep as three feet—to catch a fish. The osprey uses powerful down-strokes of its wings to resurface, and can reposition the fish in its talons once airborne. These birds do not shrink from going after "the big ones." In rare instances, ospreys have been known to drown when they tried to haul up fish that proved to be too large, and they could not release their tenacious grip.

(right) An osprey nest can weigh as much as four hundred pounds.

*Ospreys seldom venture far
from water because their diet
consists almost exclusively
of live fish.*

At first glance, an osprey can be confused with a bald eagle, another big black and white bird that fishes. However, the osprey is not as big, its wingspan is less than six feet, and it is generally white below and dark on top. An osprey tends to nab its prey under water, while the bald eagle catches fish on the surface. The two birds have calls that are somewhat similar, but the osprey's voice—a series of shrill whistles—is more audible. Ospreys are solitary hunters and don't congregate at food sources like bald eagles do.

Ospreys build large nests atop prominent features such as pine snags, rock pinnacles, and telephone poles. One such nest was found to weigh four hundred pounds. They even take advantage of man-made platforms designed specifically to attract this popular predator.

In the 1960s, ospreys were found to be falling prey themselves, in large numbers, to DDT, a pesticide sprayed on upland areas to control mosquitoes. Biologists discovered that this poison was being washed into lakes, streams, and ultimately the ocean, where it bonded with simple organisms. DDT then worked its way back up the food chain, winding up in the fish consumed by ospreys. While the pesticide did not harm the birds directly, it did interfere with their ability to produce viable eggs and offspring.

Armed with incontrovertible evidence, conservationists aggressively campaigned to outlaw the use of such toxic chemicals. Thanks to their efforts, and those of dedicated wildlife managers nationwide, osprey populations have now fully recovered.

The osprey usually hunts on the wing (above), and has reversible toes that are uniquely designed to capture slippery fish (right).

*The kite's supremacy
in the air enables it to hunt for
and capture small mammals.*

ALOFT IN THE BREEZE, a light blend of white and gray, the white-tailed kite hovers above amber grasslands that may hold the promise of a mouse. With black patches adorning the shoulders of its graceful wings, and a snow-white tail flaring wide, the white-tailed kite is a true vagabond of the American West.

Sometime during the middle of the last century, in one of the most dramatic ornithological range expansions ever documented, this kite's figurative string broke and the winds of change carried the species throughout North, Central, and South America. During this period, the white-tailed kite repopulated areas of the southern Great Plains in which it had been common a century earlier, and also expanded its range into the southeastern United States. In the American West, new regions—including areas in central and southern Arizona—were settled by pioneering pairs.

To survive in arid Arizona, which is well-populated with aerial predators such as the red-tailed hawk and Harris's hawk, the white-tailed kite has to have a behavioral advantage that enables it to coexist and compete. The kite's supremacy in the air—its ability to hover over vast expanses—enables it to hunt for and capture small mammals that a red-tailed hawk wouldn't spot from its perch on a fence post or tree limb.

In Arizona, some of the earliest nesting sites for white-tailed kites were located in abandoned agriculture fields that had large numbers of cotton rats living amidst the cover of dried and tran-sient tumbleweed. Some students of this bird believe the opening of woodlands to irrigated agriculture led to an increase in the population of small rodents, which in turn made the landscape more hospitable for the white-tailed kite. So long as there are open spaces teeming with rodents, and nest trees nearby, the white-tailed kite will be able to squeeze in among the other raptors and scratch out a living.

Wherever they reside, white-tailed kites are permanent residents and are likely to attract the attention of neighboring humans. There was a time when hawk watchers weren't quite sure what to call this kite. During the period when the species was expanding its range, scientists wondered whether there was an evolutionary relationship between kites in Africa and Australia, and those in the Americas. Kites found in various parts of the world seemed to be remarkably similar, and so scientists tended to refer to any kite anywhere as a black-shouldered kite, which is the Old World term. Finally, an expert analysis by Bill Clark and Dick Banks confirmed that the white-tailed kite of the Americas is indeed a distinct species.

*White-tailed
Kite*

Elanus leucurus

Black shoulder patches (above) adorn the graceful wings of the white-tailed kite (left).

*Only upon reaching maturity
at approximately five
years of age does this raptor
attain its "bald" head
and white tail.*

Bald Eagle

Haliaeetus leucocephalus

CHOSEN BY THE FOUNDING FATHERS on June 20, 1782, to serve as the centerpiece of the Great Seal of the United States of America, the bald eagle stands today as an enduring symbol of our nation's transcendent values of freedom, and peace through strength. To people the world over, this magnificent raptor is simply the American eagle.

With a white head and tail that contrast sharply with its blackish body and wings, which span more than seven feet, the adult bald eagle is instantly recognizable and hard to miss. Ranging from the coastline of Alaska to the desert riparian areas of Arizona, and over numerous rivers and lakes in between, bald eagles command attention wherever they are found.

The bald eagle's name refers to the color of adult bird's head: balde is Old English for "white." However, only upon reaching maturity at approximately five years of age does this raptor attain its "bald" head and white tail. When it first leaves the nest, this eagle appears dark all over and bears a greater resemblance to the golden eagle than it does to its parents. Through its fourth year, a juvenile bald eagle will be variously robed in tones and patterns of black, tawny brown, and tan.

When going after prey, bald eagles demonstrate great flying precision and coordination. They usually search for their catch from a high perch, but at times they may be seen soaring in broad circles over areas where food is most likely to be found. When a

The bald eagle's squeaky voice (above) lacks the authority one might expect from a bird chosen to serve as the centerpiece for the Great Seal of the United States of America (right).

bald eagle spots its prey, it frequently will begin its dive with an impressive roll maneuver. Unlike the osprey, a bald eagle will not plunge into the water to catch a fish. Instead, this magnificent hunter will skim the surface, sweep its legs forward, stretch its talon-tipped toes out, and stab and grab its quarry without breaking stride.

Bald eagles feed mainly on fish, and the concentrations of these birds around streams in the Pacific Northwest and Alaska during late-summer salmon runs are legendary. They also take birds, particularly waterfowl, as well as mammals. During the winter, they will consume a lot of carrion, ranging from the carcasses of livestock to road-killed rabbits.

The bald eagle and the osprey commonly occur together, and the eagle is notorious for stealing quarry from its fish-eating cousin. Typically, the bald eagle will wait for an osprey to capture a fish and drag it out of the water. Then, with a combination of direct flight and stoops onto its weary victim, the eagle will force the osprey to drop its prey and then swoop down to catch the fish before it hits the water.

Because of the bald eagle's propensity to pilfer prey and flee from attacks by much smaller birds, Benjamin Franklin thought the species was a poor choice to serve as the national bird. To him, the bald eagle was a "bird of bad moral character" and a "rank coward."

Bald eagles will construct nests in trees, except in the Southwest, where they frequently use cliff ledges. Pairs usually will produce two eggs and the young will spend about ten weeks in the

With a white head and tail that contrasts sharply with its blackish body and wings that span more than seven feet, the bald eagle is a magnificent looking raptor (left), but it does have a nasty reputation for stealing other birds' prey (above).

*The remarkable instinct of
Arizona's bald eagle fledglings
to fly north in late summer,
to places where food is most
abundant, was obviously
laid down in the DNA
of the species eons ago.*

nest before fledging. Bald eagles whose nests are disturbed will soar high and give a squeaky, chattering call that lacks the air of authority one might expect to hear from such a large and noble bird.

In most coastal areas and in the Southwest, bald eagles are permanent residents, but inland birds that nest in the north usually move south for the winter. However, researchers discovered an interesting and unexpected northward migration pattern among young Arizona-born bald eagles when they outfitted the birds with transmitters and tracked their movements. Within weeks of fledging, the eagles in the study headed north to the Pacific Northwest and Yellowstone Lake, arriving just in time to partake in the feast of spawning salmon and other fish. This remarkable instinct of Arizona's bald eagle population to fly north in late summer, to places where food is most abundant, was obviously laid down in the DNA of the species eons ago.

Once listed as endangered in the lower forty-eight states, the bald eagle was reclassified as a threatened species in 1995. The widespread use of certain pesticides after World War Two inadvertently caused bald eagles to lay eggs whose shells were too thin, and as a result bald eagle numbers declined precipitously. Now that eggshell thinning is no longer a menacing threat, populations of bald eagles nationwide are rebounding.

The prospect that the "American eagle" might actually become extinct served to galvanize public opinion and helped renew the nation's commitment to wildlife conservation. Perhaps more than with any other species, the bald eagle's recovery demonstrates that collective and concerted efforts by institutions and individuals can make a difference.

Immature bald eagles are variously robed in tones of black, tawny brown, and tan (above). During the winter (right), bald eagles will supplement their diet with livestock carcasses and road kill.

*Like owls, the northern harrier
can focus sound waves toward
its ears by ruffling the ring of feathers
that encircles its head.*

COURSING LOW over the grasslands and marshes of the American West, the northern harrier seems like just another raptor in search of a meal. In reality, this bird and a closely related South American species are unlike any other raptors on the avian family tree. In form and behavior, they are uniquely engineered.

The northern harrier is not content simply to perch and wait for prey to present itself. Instead, this enterprising bird combs the

Northern Harrier

Circus cyaneus

countryside, usually no more than ten feet above the ground, searching for small mammals, such as voles, and small birds. Like owls, the northern harrier can focus sound waves toward its ears by ruffling the ring of feathers that encircles its head. This airborne hunter has a highly developed sense of hearing and can detect the faintest rustling of prey in the grass more than ten feet away.

Their wings span four feet, and they can direct them like a sail to push themselves instantly downward in pursuit of mice and birds that they flush. If they need to inspect a grass clump before plunging in for the kill, they can hover as well. The bird also has long legs that are ideal for stabbing at prey and maneuvering on the ground, which is where they spend much of the time.

Perhaps the most unusual aspect of the northern harrier is its breeding behavior. This species nests on the ground, and a male will mate with as many as seven females. The reasons for this behavior are unclear: A polygamous male bird will tend to sire more young, but it also is true that a female which mates with a

(left) A female northern harrier will blend into the background as it combs the countryside, preying on small mammals and birds.

30

dedicated male will produce more young. Arthur Cleveland Bent, in his authoritative "Life History of North American Birds," published in 1937, made no mention of polygamy among northern harrier populations. Dr. Fran Hamerstrom, who conducted extensive surveys of northern harriers in Wisconsin in the 1960s, helped to officially document the behavior.

The male northern harrier performs an elaborate courtship display, or "sky dance," which consists of a series of sharp dives and steep ascents. A female and male initially build the nest together, and then the female lines it with fine grass to receive her eggs, which can number up to seven. Almost exclusively the female incubates them for about thirty days while the male feeds her. The young remain in the nest for about five weeks, the male providing most of the food to the female and small young. After the nestlings are about a week old the female begins to hunt also.

Female and juvenile northern harriers are a mottled brown, while the plumage of adult males is gray on back and whitish below. All northern harriers have a distinctive white rump patch at the base of their tail.

Northern harriers leave the northern portions of their breeding range in fall, and occupy grassland, marshes, open scrublands, and agricultural habitats. As the winter sun begins to set, groups of up to two dozen harriers gather on the ground, and spend the night in a communal roost. The northern harrier is truly an odd bird.

Northern harriers are polygamous, and a male (above) will mate with as many as seven females (right).

THE SHARP-SHINNED HAWK, named for the razor-like ridges on the front edges of its legs, is the epitome of stealth. As the smallest member of the genus *Accipiter,* this hawk must be fast and nimble in order to capture smaller birds on the wing while eluding its larger cousins, especially the northern goshawk, which share its preferred mixed-conifer habitat. Short wings and a long tail enable the sharp-shinned hawk to maneuver swiftly through, and nest safely in, dense forests and woodland thickets that larger predators can't penetrate.

Accipiters tend to be more excitable than hawks that inhabit more open country, and this characteristic makes them better equipped to capture their jittery prey. The sharp-shinned hawk's nervous nature also helps it evade the talons of bigger predators, particularly during the critical period of courtship and nesting, when it is most vulnerable.

In early fall, sharp-shinned hawks move from the cold north country to the warmth of more southerly latitudes, following the migrations of smaller birds. In towns and cities along the way, many will snag a meal and stay for the night. Some may choose to spend the entire winter in an urban area, preying on small birds such as nuthatches and finches.

If you hang a bird feeder outside your kitchen window in the wintertime, you too might have an unintentional, close encounter with a wild hawk. The feeder attracts just the sort of birds on which the sharp-shinned hawk preys. Sometimes, this lovely little hawk will accidentally hit the window glass with enough force to

Sharp-shinned Hawk

Accipiter striatus

break its neck, in which case recovering the lifeless body is a truly sad event. More often, such a collision will leave the bird momentarily stunned and it will fly away as soon as it can. If the survivor is unable to fly when approached, it most likely has a bruised or broken wing that will require rehabilitation.

Ironically, this all-too-common scenario provides bird lovers with one of the best opportunities to see this magnificent and beautiful creature up close. The plumage of the adult sharp-shinned hawk—deep blue-gray on the back and rufous on the underside—is awe inspiring enough to win the hearts and minds of any bird lover, even those whose backyard feeders have been targeted by this predatory opportunist.

The mottled plumage of the juvenile sharp-shinned hawk (left) turns rufous on the underside and a deep blue-gray on the back as the bird reaches maturity (below).

> The sharp-shinned hawk's nervous nature helps it evade the talons of bigger predators.

*When searching for prey,
the Cooper's hawk often stands
still and upright with its long tail
trailing straight down.*

Cooper's Hawk

Accipiter cooperii

DARTING AMONG THE TRUNKS of tall trees, a Cooper's hawk swoops up and lands on a rugged, low branch of an ancient oak tree. It grabs on with such force that the old limb sways and groans. Then it hunches and rubs its beak on the bark. Loose pieces rain down on the leaves below. A few quick glances around and it's off again in search of a more secluded place to preen its plumage and digest its meal.

Such is the after-breakfast routine of the Cooper's hawk. The same scene plays out time and again in woodlands, forests, and urban landscapes throughout the West.

When searching for prey, the Cooper's hawk often stands still and upright with one foot raised and tucked under its fluffed belly feathers and its long tail trailing straight down. The only thing that moves is its head, which it turns with abrupt jerks in the direction of any motion it detects that might signal the presence of a bird or small mammal.

Like its other *Accipiter* cousins, the northern goshawk and sharp-shinned hawk, the Cooper's hawk is well-equipped to make a quick dash for quarry in brushy terrain. But unlike these other raptors, the Cooper's hawk frequently will nest in towns and cities. I have witnessed the dramatic courtship flights of the Cooper's hawk over a park in the very center of a large Western

(above and right) The Cooper's hawk is one of the most adaptable and resilient raptors, and is at home in a wider range of habitats than any other Accipiter species.

city. When courting, this beautiful bird flies straight, making deep, slow, and exaggerated wingbeats and flaring its tail coverts in a signal of territoriality.

A Cooper's hawk pair builds its nest with wispy, dead limbs that the birds pull loose and carry in their beaks to the canopy of a tree. They usually line the nest with bark. Urban nests are easily discovered by the *cack-cack-cack-cack* defensive call that adults make, and by the ring of "white-wash" below, formed by the excrement of well fed nestlings.

The Cooper's hawk has a habit of taking prey to a "butcher bloc"—a horizontal limb or stump somewhere near the nest—where it plucks the catch and frequently consumes the head prior to taking the remains to its young. A study of animal remains at these sites reveals the variety of this hawk's diet, which consists mainly of birds, but also includes small mammals and lizards.

After fledglings leave the nest, and before they realize they are now on their own, they instinctively will continue to scream for food from their parents. In the forest, this vocalizing may sound wild and wonderful, but in your neighborhood is can be downright annoying.

In late summer, Cooper's hawks leave their summer homes in the mountains and northlands of the American West and head to warmer country, where they may encounter year-round-resident hawks that do not appreciate the arrival of "snowbird" competitors. Migrant Cooper's hawks return to breeding areas in the north in March, setting up their nurseries with all the noise and flutter so characteristic of birds in spring.

Of the three *Accipiter* species, the Cooper's hawk has the greatest flexibility in its choice of nesting habitats and is at home in the widest range of ecosystems. I have found nests in town, in conifer trees in the cool mountains, and in palo verde trees in the hot Sonoran Desert. The Cooper's hawk is truly one of the most adaptable and resilient raptors of all.

(left) A Cooper's hawk will spread its wings to mantle prey from the view of other predators.

WHETHER STREAKING THROUGH THE FOREST as a big, gray blur or perched stealthily on a tree limb, its dusky head accented by a white swoosh above each glaring red eye, the northern goshawk is an unforgettable sight.

With wings that span nearly four feet, this large raptor is capable of great bursts of speed. Its exceptionally long tail helps it dart around dense vegetation to overtake smaller birds and mammals that might otherwise evade its grasp. These characteristics make the northern goshawk the bird of choice for many falconers.

More so than the closely related Cooper's hawk and sharp-shinned hawk, the northern goshawk prefers to feed on small mammals, which can comprise fifty percent of the bird's diet in some regions of the American West. Like most other raptors, the northern goshawk uses its broad wings to mantle, or shield, captured prey from the view of potential rivals. Ironically, other raptors instinctively interpret the sight of a hawk mantling prey as a sure sign that it has caught something.

Once, while hiking in a mountain meadow in southeastern New Mexico, I saw a northern goshawk capture a common flicker. The goshawk immediately covered its prize with a shroud of outstretched wings. Through my binoculars, I watched as it looked around furtively, and with good reason.

Within thirty seconds, an adult red-tailed hawk appeared and quickly made for the grounded goshawk. The northern goshawk attempted to carry off the flicker, but with the added weight in its talons there was no way it could escape the pirate hawk. Lest the smaller predator become prey itself, it dropped the flicker within one hundred feet of where it had made the kill. The red-tailed hawk pounced on the lifeless flicker and quickly mantled its booty from other would-be thieves.

Northern goshawks occur in sub-arctic and northern temperate regions, and they prefer to nest in extensive stands of large,

Northern Goshawk

Accipiter gentilis

"old growth" trees. In the American West, the northern goshawk's biggest competitor is the logging industry. The management challenge has been to preserve sufficient critical habitat for the northern goshawk while maintaining ecologically sensible and economically important timber harvest programs. Since the late 1980s, a substantial amount of scientific study, lobbying, and legal wrangling has focused on the habitat needs of this particular species.

Northern goshawks usually nest in the largest trees, and they defend their territory very aggressively. An adult will issue a series of loud, high-pitched *ki-ki-ki-ki* calls if man or beast should venture too close to its nest, and will not hesitate to strike a trespasser with its open talons. Some even have been known to grab on and inflict serious puncture wounds. The northern goshawk female will lay an average of three eggs, which she will incubate for about thirty-four days. Five to six weeks after birth, the young birds are on the wing.

Each fall, northern goshawks migrate to regions where prey will be more plentiful during the winter months. As they make their way south, they are more apt to stray from their typical forest cover. For those fortunate enough to encounter one, a northern goshawk will leave a lasting impression.

Having captured its quarry (left), the northern goshawk will instinctively shield it from the prying eyes of competitors (above).

In October, the entire Arizona gray hawk population migrates to northern Mexico.

ITS VOICE CAPTURES ONE'S ATTENTION, its flight intrigues, and its striking beauty captivates. Every spring and summer, in hopes of glimpsing the gray hawk, thousands of birdwatchers converge on southeastern Arizona, the northern edge of this magnificent bird's range.

One of the most vocal raptors in the West, the gray hawk has a cry similar to that of a peacock. Its distinctive flight pattern, consisting of quick wing beats followed by a glide, is an evolutionary adaptation characteristic of forest-dwelling hawks. The prominent barred, gray and white breast and black and white tail are attractive, but it is the gray hawk's black eye and yellow, fleshy cere above the bill that birders find most awe-inspiring.

Gray Hawk

Asturina nitida

Preferred habitat for nesting north of the border is lush riparian areas with plenty of cottonwood trees, bordered by bosques of giant mesquite. About mid-March, gray hawks migrate to southeastern Arizona from their wintering grounds in Mexico and begin to build nests as soon as they arrive.

Not particularly fearful of humans, some gray hawk pairs have been known to nest in the yards of rural dwellings near Patagonia and Nogales, Arizona, and their vocal and aerial courtship displays entertain residents and neighbors, alike. Elsewhere in southeastern Arizona, The Nature Conservancy's Patagonia-Sonoita Creek Preserve, and the Bureau of Land Management's San Pedro National Conservation Area, are the most popular places for the public to view this raptor.

Spiny lizards and whiptail lizards are favorite prey. I once watched three hungry, half-grown gray hawks battle for an eight-inch whiptail that one of the parents had dropped onto the nest.

(right) The gray hawk is one of the most vocal raptors in the American West and has a cry similar to that of a peacock.

One of the eager chicks grabbed the flopping lizard and turned away from its siblings to swallow it head-first. When the satiated victor turned around, about an inch of wiggling lizard tail was still hanging from its beak. The sight of those hungry nest mates, all bobbing and weaving as each tried to grab on to the whipping tail, was very amusing.

By the time fledgling gray hawks are ready to leave the nest, sometime in July, their body coloration is a streaked brown and buff. This juvenile color pattern is quite different from that of the adult bird. In October, the entire Arizona gray hawk population migrates to northern Mexico, and in particular to the low coastal woodlands and foothills of the Sierra Madre, where the species is one of the most commonly encountered hawks.

Hundreds of years ago, gray hawks were abundant along the Santa Cruz River near Tucson, Arizona. Climate change and population growth in the early and mid 1900s permanently altered the character of this area. What was once a perennially flowing stream lined with cottonwoods is today a dry river course virtually denuded of trees.

In the early 1970s ornithologists counted fewer than fifty gray hawk pairs in Arizona. Today, the population totals nearly one hundred nesting pairs. This dramatic increase is a credit to more responsible stewardship by both private landowners and the state government, which has acquired and is managing important breeding areas in Arizona.

These concerted efforts will ensure that, for generations to come, the unmistakable call of the gray hawk will resound in the wooded river valleys and canyons of southeastern Arizona, lifting the spirits of all who hear it.

The plumage of a fledgling gray hawk is a streaked brown and buff (left), while the adult bird's barred, gray and white breast and black and white tail make it easily identifiable in flight (above).

Its distinctive flight pattern, consisting of quick wing beats followed by a glide, is an evolutionary adaptation characteristic of forest-dwelling hawks.

*Common black-hawks are
exceptionally protective parents
and will sit for hours to shade offspring
from the hot midday sun.*

I T'S SPRINGTIME IN SOUTHEASTERN ARIZONA. Deep
within a remote canyon, a crystalline stream burbles over a bed
of cobbled stones. Large, thirsty cottonwood and sycamore trees
line the banks, and their branches form a restful, shady canopy.
Here and there, patches of bright blue sky peak through, and
shafts of bright sunlight alternate with leafy shadows to create a
dappled quilt below. Cheerful birdsongs blend with the soft sounds
of flowing water and rustling leaves. Otherwise, in this place of
solitude and serenity, all is quiet.

Then, the silence is shattered by a burst of piercing whistles,
more like screams, which continues for several seconds before
tapering off. I am no longer alone.
This is prime breeding territory for
North America's most thrilling raptor,
the common black-hawk.

Common Black-Hawk
Buteogallus anthracinus

Despite its "common" name, there
is nothing mundane about this bird.
Genetically, it is descended from the
solitary eagle and crowned eagle of
Central and South America. The common black-hawk is a big bird:
its broad wings span four feet and when folded they hide much of
the tail, which has a distinguishing, wide white band.

Unlike most other raptors in the West (except the osprey,
bald eagle, and red-shouldered hawk) the common black-hawk
has a diet that consists mostly of fish and frogs. Aquatic insects,
small mammals, nestling birds, snakes, and lizards round out the
menu. When hunting, it may choose a low perch from which to
pounce on prey in shallow water, or it may wade along the edges
of the stream and grab prey with its feet.

To maintain its plumage, the common black-hawk will lie on
a sandy bank in the sun, breast-down with wings and tail spread,

*(right) Common black-hawks will construct substantial nests in large trees
along perennial waterways.*

The common black-hawk
has a diet that consists mostly
of fish and frogs.

and then preen its flight and body feathers. This is a necessary, daily ritual for a bird that invariably gets wet while hunting.

Common black-hawks are absent from the United States during the fall and winter, preferring to spend those months in Mexico, closer to their neo-tropical cousins. In March, those at the northern fringe of the range return to nesting grounds in central and southern Arizona and southwestern New Mexico. There they construct substantial nests in large trees along perennial waterways.

Clutch size usually is two eggs, which hatch in about thirty-eight days. Common black-hawks are exceptionally protective parents and will sit for hours to shade offspring from the hot mid-day sun. Once, while conducting a field study with Dr. Robert Ohmart of Arizona State University, I was about to remove young birds from the nest—in order to measure and band them—when a defensive parent flew swiftly and silently inches from my head and almost knocked me from the tree.

The common black-hawk will instinctively take to the air in noisy protest when anyone intrudes on its territory. This can be problematic for those that choose to nest near popular recreational areas, because the imperative to defend the nest will distract the birds from shading and feeding their nestlings. Fortunately, most of the two hundred or so prime nesting areas in Arizona and New Mexico are located on more remote public lands, where access is carefully managed. This ensures that most common black-hawk young will fledge successfully. Thus, this impressive bird will continue to inhabit the rugged, tucked-away riparian areas of the American Southwest.

(left) The common black-hawk's wings span four feet and hide much of its tail when folded.

commonly she will opt to have two mates plus another nest attendant, which often is an immature bird. These extra males assist harmoniously in building the nest, guarding the eggs, feeding the female and young, and defending the territory against other raptors. Observations, confirmed by DNA analysis, indicate that the dominant female will copulate with both adult males. Harris's hawks breed almost year round in the deserts of southern Arizona, and some nesting groups raise as many as three broods in a single year.

In Arizona, the breeding range of the Harris's hawk appears to be expanding, and the bird is increasingly seen nesting in urban settings. With a big white rump patch accenting its charcoal body and splashes of chestnut on its thighs and shoulders, this bird is a visual delight for the backyard birder. In Tucson, Arizona, clusters of this raptor have been observed cruising golf courses, desert washes, and other refuges of open space. They feed on quail and cottontails and have learned that pigeons like to nest in the fronds of urban, non-native palm trees.

Perhaps the greatest risk the Harris's hawk faces is electrocution from power lines. The electric utility industry diligently studied this problem and responded with new configurations for utility poles, which minimize the chance that the wings of landing raptors will come in contact with transmission wires.

Despite its forays into the urban jungle, the Harris's hawk is still most at home in the unspoiled expanses of the Sonoran desert. Perched atop a stately saguaro, a black silhouette against an ochre sky, this most sociable of hawks surveys a sea of cacti and patiently waits for its nest mates to flush the evening meal.

Harris's hawks breed almost year round in southern Arizona (left), and have evolved an array of ritualized postures to communicate intent (right).

*Perhaps more than any other hawk, the Swainson's hawk
exhibits a variety of colors and patterns of plumage.*

DUST FROM A FAR AWAY LAND: that's what I pondered after releasing a Swainson's hawk I had trapped late one March afternoon in the Sulphur Springs Valley of southeastern Arizona. The birds were just passing through in large waves from the south, and as part of a study on raptor migration I had placed a band on the leg of this particular hawk in hopes that I might eventually learn more about the course of her journey.

I examined her relatively small feet and thought about all the grasshoppers they must have snagged last fall when she previously passed through this valley, headed in the opposite direction. There was a small glob of dried dirt stuck between the pad of her foot and the joint of her middle toe. I absent-mindedly rubbed off the dirt with my finger before releasing her to rejoin perhaps fifty or more other Swainson's soaring overhead.

Only later, when I noticed that the dirt was still on my finger, did I muse as to its origin. Could that smudge contain soil from the flat and windy grasslands of Argentina, six thousand miles to the south, where my brief captive had spent the winter? If I had not bothered to clean it off, would that clod have hung on all the way to Canada or even eastern Alaska, where by April my banded friend might be defending her nest? It was certainly possible.

Swainson's Hawk

Buteo swainsoni

Swainson's hawks breed exclusively in grasslands and scrublands west of the Mississippi, and winter in the grasslands of Argentina. Migrating such long distances is not without peril, but researchers recently determined that the greatest threats to this raptor exist on its wintering grounds.

In the early 1990s Brian Woodbridge, a biologist in California, used global positioning satellite transmitters to track the migration of two Swainson's hawks to alfalfa and sunflower fields in Argentina. He was horrified by what he discovered there: the ground was littered with thousands of dead hawks. Large expanses of the pampas grasslands had been cultivated, and insecticides had been used liberally to control marauding grasshoppers.

What followed is perhaps one of the greatest success stories in the history of raptor conservation. An international effort was launched to document Swainson's hawk migration patterns, and researchers presented their findings to governments, chemical companies, and farmers. As a result, Argentine farmers now use safer chemicals to control insect problems and the hawks have staged a remarkable comeback.

(left) Even as a juvenile, the Swainson's hawk is best recognized by the pointed shape of its wings.

At a nest in Arizona,
I once found remains
of a collared lizard,
a whiptail lizard,
and the spiny, inedible
heads of sixteen
horned lizards.

In addition to grasshoppers and other insects, Swainson's hawks prey on small mammals, birds, and reptiles. At a nest in Arizona, I once found remains of a collared lizard, a whiptail lizard, and the spiny, inedible heads of sixteen horned lizards. During August, when grasshopper populations erupt on Western rangelands, Swainson's hawks begin to gather in small groups. In agricultural areas, they will swarm behind harvesters and feast on insects and mammals that are uncovered in their wake.

Swainson's hawks are best recognized by the pointed shape of their wings, not by their color patterns. Perhaps more than any other hawk, the Swainson's hawk exhibits a variety of colors and patterns of plumage. This makes them difficult for novice hawk-watchers to recognize. But if you should see clusters of raptors on the move over the open landscapes of the American West in the spring and fall, they could well be Swainson's hawks.

Migrating through southeastern Arizona, Swainson's hawks will pause to feed on the area's abundant supply of grasshoppers (above), and some will even choose to nest in the nearby Sulphur Springs Valley (left).

IS THAT BIG BLACK SOARING BIRD a turkey vulture, a common black-hawk, or some other mysterious raptor in melanistic plumage? Birders in the Southwest need to take a closer look because it could be the seldom-seen zone-tailed hawk.

At first glance, this bird is commonly misidentified because it resembles the turkey vulture in so many ways. Like the turkey vulture, the zone-tailed hawk is basically black. This is true even of fledglings, which do not have the brown-streaked feathering typical of other young raptors. Only when the zone-tailed hawk spreads its tail feathers is its diagnostic, grayish white band or "zone" revealed.

Even in flight, the zone-tailed hawk mimics the turkey vulture, with a rocking motion that appears unstable and wings forming the characteristic "v"-shaped dihedral. With a wingspan of up to fifty-five inches, the zone-tailed hawk is smaller than the average vulture. This size difference makes the hawk appear to be farther away to unsuspecting small birds, mammals, and lizards.

Whether fooling prey or people, the zone-tailed hawk is a very successful avian predator in its remote canyon and mountain

haunts of Arizona and New Mexico, where it breeds during spring and summer. It nests in large riparian trees like cottonwood and sycamore, and in pine and fir trees higher in the mountains. Common clutch size is two eggs, which the female incubates for about thirty-five days.

Zone-tailed hawks defend their nests with great vigor. Near Patagonia, Arizona, I once photographed an adult bird, famous for its nest guardianship, as it smacked the head of hawk researcher Jim Dawson, who was walking toward the nest tree.

Zone-tailed Hawk

Buteo albonotatus

It seems that people have been recording interesting encounters with the zone-tailed hawk ever since the mid 1800s, when it was discovered in the West by pioneer scientists. One of the most famous of these events was documented by Major Charles Bendire, who in the 1870s was stationed at Fort Lowell near Tucson, Arizona, to help quell Apache raids. One day, Major Bendire rode to a nearby canyon, where he climbed up a cottonwood tree to collect an egg from a zone-tailed hawk nest. From that privileged vantage point, he was astonished to spot a band of Apaches, who were likewise surprised to see him. Putting the interests of science before his own personal safety, the major gently placed the egg in his mouth and carefully climbed down the tree. Then, he quickly mounted his horse and covered the five miles back to the fort as fast as he could, without breaking the egg, of course.

In flight, the zone-tailed hawk mimics the turkey vulture and can fool unsuspecting prey, including lizards (above). Certain distinguishing marks, such as the bands on the tail feathers of this juvenile (right), may be discerned only on closer inspection.

The red-tailed hawk occurs throughout all ecological zones of the West, from the dry deserts of the Southwest to the moist sub-arctic conifer forests of Alaska.

DRIVE ALONG A RURAL ROAD lined with telephone poles and sooner or later you probably will spot a hawk perched on one, scanning the countryside for potential prey. Chances are the bird will be the ubiquitous red-tailed hawk.

Red-tailed Hawk

Buteo jamaicensis

Although it is the most commonly encountered hawk in the American West, the red-tailed hawk is also one of the most difficult to identify. It seems as if no two red-tailed hawks are alike. In the western United States, in particular, they appear in a multitude of colors, from blackish chocolate through reddish brown. Even some partial albinos have been reported.

The "typical" red-tailed hawk, if there is such a thing, has a light breast with a swath of darker coloration below. From the back, the bird appears dark brown with two distinctive buffy shoulder patches. No matter the garb, all red-tailed hawks two years or older will sport a reddish brown tail. Tails of juveniles, which are barred with shades of brown and buff, resemble those

(left) The "typical" red-tailed hawk, if there is such a thing, has a light breast with a swath of darker coloration below, but in the American West it is not uncommon to see them in a variety of guises.

of many other young hawks. The sight of a red-tailed hawk can leave many novice birders wondering why no picture in their field guides matches the hawk they see on that pole.

The red-tailed hawk occurs throughout all ecological zones of the West, from the dry deserts of the Southwest to the moist sub-arctic conifer forests of Alaska. It is an enterprising bird that seems to thrive just about everywhere. Most red-tailed hawks remain within their breeding territories throughout the year, but some birds in northern regions and at higher elevations, where significant snowfall covers the landscape in winter, do get the urge to migrate south.

This large raptor has broad wings that are ideal for soaring and hovering over any habitat, and it can snatch a mouse scurrying through a desert wash as easily as it can grab a squirrel climbing a ponderosa pine tree. If the winds are just right, the red-tailed

The red-tailed hawk has broad wings (above), and its piercing eyes can detect the slightest movement of prey (right).

In May, as saguaros in the Sonoran Desert begin to bloom, fledgling hawks there are ready to leave the nest.

hawk can fly to a fixed point along a ridge and maintain its position by controlling the air flow around its body with minute wing and tail movements, all the while keeping its head perfectly still. Scanning the slope, its piercing eyes can detect the slightest movement of prey. But if nothing is available below, the red-tailed hawk merely gestures its wingtips and slips along the ridge to another aerial lookout.

In the Southwestern deserts, where mated pairs are permanent residents, courtship begins in early January. While northern climes are deep in the grip of winter, the Sonoran Desert is alive with activity. The winter sun warms the desert floor and by late morning the air begins to stir. Courting pairs of hawks catch these breezes and ascend in slow, gentle circles. The male stays above his mate, descending frequently and lowering both legs as though he were trying to land on his mate's back. The pair eventually swoops down together, often landing on the trunk or arm of a saguaro cactus. There they'll perch or copulate. Then, together, they will gather dry mesquite, palo verde, and creosote branches from the desert floor to refurbish last season's nest. That is, if a great horned owl pair hasn't usurped it for their own use.

In May, as saguaros in the Sonoran Desert begin to bloom, fledgling hawks there are ready to leave the nest. Meanwhile, in Alaska, red-tailed hawks are just beginning to see their broods emerge from their eggs.

In the Sonoran Desert, red-tailed hawks mate in January and will construct substantial nests, often in the arms of a giant saguaro cactus (left). By June, juveniles are fending for themselves (above).

*It hunts most often from
the air, soaring on great
white wings that span
an impressive five feet.*

THE LARGEST HAWK IN NORTH AMERICA prefers to live the life of a reclusive gypsy, shunning cultivated and developed landscapes in favor of the rugged and forbidding back-o-beyond. But as the once-vast rangelands and unpopulated regions of the American West continue to shrink, the wild isolation that the ferruginous hawk craves is getting harder to find.

This hawk, which has the smallest breeding range of any widely occurring North American hawk, is exceedingly sensitive to the immediate presence of humans and almost always chooses to nest where people aren't. However, the ferruginous hawk isn't shy about nesting on man-made objects such as transmission line towers, windmills, and rock or masonry chimneys of abandoned farm houses. Farther afield, it will nest on rocky outcrops, and even on the ground.

Ferruginous Hawk
Buteo regalis

A ferruginous hawk pair will build a huge nest, using lots of dead tree branches and even sun-bleached bones. This species also has the curious habit of lining nests with the dried dung of livestock. As a general rule, larger raptors lay fewer eggs, but that does not apply to the ferruginous hawk. Its clutch may consist of as many as eight eggs. Because this hawk depends upon native habitats and natural prey cycles, it may skip a breeding season if natural food sources become scarce.

(right) The ferruginous hawk appears in a variety of plumage colors, including the light morph of this juvenile.

The ferruginous hawk preys almost exclusively on medium-size mammals. Jackrabbits are a favorite item. It hunts most often from the air, soaring on great white wings that span an impressive five feet, or hovering over towns of prairie dogs and ground squirrels. Alternatively, and usually at dawn or dusk, the ferruginous hawk will pick a perch from which to spot prey, and then streak close to the ground in pursuit with slow, strong wingbeats.

This bird has a very wide gape and can swallow some smaller prey whole. One winter I came upon a dead ferruginous hawk in an alfalfa field. When I opened its stomach to study the contents, I discovered an intact pocket gopher.

Like other raptors that live in open country, the ferruginous hawk appears in a variety of plumage colors, ranging from light to dark brown and rufous. The common name is a derivative of *ferrugo*, the Latin word for rust, which is appropriate because adult ferruginous hawks are rusty or dark brown above and very light below. The shoulders and thighs of adult birds also are a rusty brown.

Some conservationists fear that this bird will not be able to cope with the rapid pace of urbanization in the American West, but so long as there remain landscapes too bleak for humans to inhabit, the ferruginous hawk will remain a sentinel of the West, and a reminder of the need to preserve those wild places.

The term "ferruginous" is derived from the Latin word for rust, which is appropriate because adult ferruginous hawks are rusty brown above and have a very light breast (below). Juveniles have light patches on their outer wings (left).

The wild isolation that the ferruginous hawk craves is getting harder to find.

This resilient raptor overshadows the national symbol in one undeniable aspect: The golden eagle is America's largest bird of prey.

Golden Eagle

Aquila chrysaetos

RECLUSIVE INHABITANT OF CRAGGY MOUNTAINS and windswept plains throughout the northern hemisphere, the golden eagle is perhaps most at home in the American West—a region of unparalleled biological diversity, where ecosystems range from cool, pine-forested mountains to hot, sparsely vegetated deserts. Seldom seen and long misunderstood, this resilient raptor overshadows the national symbol in one undeniable aspect: The golden eagle is America's largest "true" bird of prey.

Yellowish feathers crown the head of this magnificent eagle, and these feathers become more distinctive and "golden" as the bird matures. Otherwise, the golden eagle's plumage is predominantly dark brown, with light patches on the tail and wings, which span more than seven feet. The golden eagle can soar for miles, at great heights, and then swiftly dive to snatch an unsuspecting prairie dog, jackrabbit, javelina, or bull snake in its massive talons. This bird also can subdue larger prey, such as young deer and antelope.

The golden eagle will supplement its diet of live prey by scavenging, and will aggressively assert its prerogative to a free meal. Vultures must wait their turn.

(right) Golden eagles erect their nests on rocky cliffs and outcrops, and in trees on mountain slopes.

The number of young that a nesting pair of golden eagles rears in any given year will vary according to the availability of important prey.

During the mid 1900s, farmers and ranchers throughout the American West sought to eradicate golden eagles in the mistaken belief that these large, powerful predators were responsible for killing their livestock. During a twenty-year period beginning in the late 1940s, more than twenty thousand golden eagles were exterminated in the United States. Subsequent field studies revealed that, in almost every case, suspect birds were feeding on lambs and calves that had died of natural causes. Evidence also showed that domesticated animals—live or dead—were not common in the golden eagle's diet. Armed with this data, wildlife officials intervened to stop the slaughter.

Golden eagles erect their nests on rocky cliffs and outcrops, and in trees on mountain slopes. Typically, a female will lay two or three eggs several days apart, and incubate them for as long as forty-five days. The chick that hatches first invariably gets the largest share of the food ration. When food is scarce, the first-born will fill its belly and sometimes even kill its siblings.

Eaglets leave the nest in six to eight weeks, and the number of young that a nesting pair rears in any given year will vary according to the availability of important prey.

During the fall and winter, eagles from northern latitudes move south to more moderate climates and gather in valleys where prey populations are abundant. Unlike bald eagles, golden eagles do not form large, conspicuous congregations.

Where once they were unfairly persecuted, golden eagle populations in many parts of the American West are actually increasing today. Protected by wildlife laws and appreciated by a growing number of enlightened and conservation-minded Americans, the golden eagle's future is assured.

The golden eagle female (above) will lay two or three eggs several days apart, and when food is scarce the first-born (left) will fill its belly and sometimes even kill its siblings.

The crested caracara's long,
yellow legs enable it to pursue lizards,
small mammals, and hatchling quail.

T HEY RESIDE IN THE SHADOW of Baboquivari, a mystical mountain that is sacred to the Tohono O'odham people of southern Arizona and northern Sonora, Mexico. The origin story and spiritual life of the people revolve around this monolith, which rises nearly five thousand feet above the adjoining desert, scrub, and grassland. Indirectly, the colorful caracara is a beneficiary of Tohono O'odham lifeways.

Crested caracaras survive in part by scavenging carcasses, On the Tohono O'odham Nation these birds find plenty of carrion on which to feast because livestock which die a natural death there are left for wildlife to consume. Also, Tohono O'odham livestock watering holes provide crested caracaras with their only source of moisture during the hot and dry Sonoran Desert summers. These factors help explain

Crested Caracara

Caracara cheriway

why crested caracaras are more common in the Arizona-Mexico borderlands now than they were a century ago.

The crested caracara can grab an easy breakfast by cruising above roadways and picking up the previous night's roadkill. In order to compete with vultures, which cannot soar until air thermals develop, the crested caracara knows to get up early.

This bird also is an able hunter of live prey. The Levy brothers, who conducted the only study of this species in the West, found that crested caracaras are particularly fond of horned lizards.

(left) The crested caracara survives in part by scavenging carcasses, but it also is an able hunter of live prey.

Crested caracaras will hunt for prey on the ground (right) or from a superior vantage point (above).

The bird's long, yellow legs enable it to pursue lizards, small mammals, and hatchling quail. As the crested caracara walks and hops on the ground, it pokes its head into places that may harbor a bird nest, and frequently is rewarded by a meal of eggs.

In mid-March, a crested caracara pair will begin to construct a nest of fine twigs in the arms of a saguaro cactus. They will reuse their old nest if it has not been taken over by another raptor, such as a great horned owl, red-tailed hawk, or Harris's hawk.

The food that parents regurgitate to feed their hatchlings is often the putrid remains of a carcass. Eventually the offspring graduate to solid food: dismembered pieces of prey captured live.

For the crested caracara, a saguaro also serves as an ideal sentinel perch. The giant cactus towers over every other form of desert vegetation, and it is common to see a crested caracara watch for prey and predators from this superior vantage point. Even if you don't see the bird, a saguaro topped with a tell-tale whitewash of waste material is a sure sign that crested caracaras are nesting nearby.

In the United States, the crested caracara also can be found in central and southern Florida and south Texas, but in numbers so few that it is considered rare and threatened. South of the border, the bird is so common that it is has been dubbed the Mexican eagle and appears—gripping a snake—on that country's national seal and flag.

The crested caracara's range extends as far south as the tip of South America, so why is its range in the United States so limited? Clearly, it prefers open or semi-open country, either arid or well watered, and there is plenty of that sort of territory north of the border. One would think that, if the crested caracara is hearty enough to survive on the windy moors of Argentina's Patagonia and Isla Grande, it would also be found on the Great Plains of North America. The fact that it is not remains one of the great mysteries of avian biogeography.

Perhaps clues to the answer can be found in the relationship the crested caracara forms not only with the climate and the land, but also with the people who reside there. People like the Tohono O'odham, who accommodate the crested caracara and accept the role it plays in the circle of life.

DESPITE ITS FLAMBOYANT AND PUGNACIOUS NATURE, the American kestrel is actually the smallest falcon in the American West. In fact, in the entire world, only the Seychelles kestrel, which inhabits a remote chain of islands in the Indian Ocean, is smaller. But don't underestimate this little bird. What the American kestral lacks in size the male of the species more than makes up for in color and tenacity.

American Kestrel
Falco sparverius

With most bird species, the male is significantly larger (and in many cases more colorful) than the female. For nearly all birds of prey, however, this dimorphic (meaning "two forms") condition is reversed: the female is larger than the male of the same species. Kestrels are the exception. The disparity in size between the adult female American kestrel and the adult male is almost imperceptible, but the difference in their plumage is dramatic.

The wings of the adult male American kestrel are a striking blue and contrast beautifully with the rich rufous hues on its back and tail. With colors of only buff and brown, females look comparatively drab. Perched together, male and female American kestrels look as though they could be two entirely different species.

The function of reverse sexual dimorphism in raptors has been a topic of much scientific discussion, and the reasons for the

The male American kestrel's striking blue wings contrast with the rufous hues on its back and tail (left), while the buff and brown female looks comparatively drab (right).

color difference in the American kestrel are just as curious. Also interesting is the fact that, unlike every other kestrel species in the world, American kestrel fledglings mirror their parents from the time they leave the nest.

The American kestrel is perhaps the most common bird of prey in the West. From central Alaska to the tip of South America, this species inhabits wide open country in typical falcon fashion. The American kestrel feeds on a variety of prey, including insects, small mammals, birds, and lizards as big as the thirteen-inch-long desert spiny.

Sometimes called "sparrow hawk," the American kestrel has the temperament and ability to take more than just sparrows. I once witnessed a male, on the ground, struggling to kill an adult mourning dove. Its prey fought furiously, flapping it wings and bouncing around, but the raptor had the dove's head in a death

*The American kestrel is perhaps
the most common bird of prey
in the West.*

grip and was not about to let go. Eventually, the determined American kestrel succeeded in killing its prey. After eating part of the dove, it flew off with a portion of the legs to stash for a future meal.

The American kestrel will either perch and wait for prey or search by hovering. Even with the slightest of breezes, the kestrel can hold its position over a likely food source by rapidly flapping its wings and spreading its tail. Once it spots its quarry, the little falcon will dive straight down and then spread its wings and tail right before it grabs its prey.

American kestrels usually nest in cavities that have been created by other birds in trees or cacti, and in rare instances they will use cliff potholes. This bird is also receptive to making a home in a man-made nest box, particularly if that box is situated in open areas near plenty of prey. Wherever it resides, the cantankerous American kestrel never fails to attract attention.

American kestrels usually nest in cavities created by other birds in trees or cacti (above), and feed on a variety of prey, including mice (right).

I F E V E R T H E R E W A S A F A L C O N that behaved more like a hawk, it is the Merlin. In many ways, this little falcon acts like the forest-dwelling sharp-shinned hawk, which occupies an entirely different branch of the avian family tree. Like the sharp-shined hawk, the merlin sneaks up on its quarry by flying very low to the ground, using the contour of the terrain for concealment. The association doesn't end there: falcon expert Tom Cade also has observed the two species hunting and migrating together.

For a bird-eating raptor with a holarctic distribution, the merlin ought to be more common, but it is relatively rare. Sightings can be difficult to confirm because there are three geographically distinct subspecies of merlin in the West, and for each the colorations of the male and female are markedly different. Adult birds of the subspecies that nests in the dense conifer forests along the Pacific Northwest and Alaskan coasts have dark plumage. The merlin subspecies that inhabits the open prairies has a lighter color scheme more in keeping with its habitat, but in this case the difference between male and female plumage is much greater.

This unusual falcon has a penchant for nesting in forests and woodlands adjacent to open areas with grassy cover, and it uses

Merlin

*Falco
columbarius*

tree perches to spot game prior to pursuing it. When racing over wide sand bars and open shallows while migrating along the coast, the merlin displays its true falcon nature. In mid-flight it can swoop down and scoop up any small to medium-sized bird that has momentarily let down its guard. Merlins migrate over great distances, traveling all the way to South America, and wintering along the northwestern coast of that continent. In March, merlins return to their North American breeding grounds, which are scattered from Wyoming north throughout Canada and much of Alaska.

These birds establish pair bonds with vocalizations and courtship displays of aerial acrobatics. The male also will present a symbolic offering of food to the female, an act that often concludes with copulation. Merlins prefer to use old nests built by other birds in the dense canopy of tall trees, and sometimes they will line these nests with greenery gathered from surrounding trees. Where trees are absent but prey is plentiful, merlins occasionally will nest on the ground.

Since the early 1970s, increasing numbers of merlins have been choosing to nest and over-winter in cities on the Canadian prairie, where they can find an abundant assortment of prey and nesting substrate. In Saskatoon, Saskatchewan, for example, trees planted as part of a civic landscaping plan initially served as nesting sites for crows, but merlins have now largely displaced the original nest builders. Also, the understory of ornamental plants now teems with urban quarry sufficient to support a growing year-round merlin population. City planners may have intended only to beautify the city setting for people, but the scheme wound up creating a very attractive urban habitat for the merlin too.

The merlin uses tree perches to spot game (left), and will sneak up on its quarry by flying very low to the ground (right).

Big, strong, and blessed with powerful wings,
the gyrfalcon dominates most birds and
small mammals that inhabit the Arctic.

THE LARGEST FALCON ON THE PLANET presides at the top of the world. Seldom seen in its natural domain, the gyrfalcon is a regal bird fit for a king. Falconry literature is replete with tales of this magnificent bird's powers of flight, especially its ability to climb with blinding speed, like a missile, and to overtake any quarry with ease in level, hot pursuit. Little wonder that captive gyrfalcons were bred and trained to hunt exclusively from the royal fist.

Big, strong, and blessed with powerful wings, the gyrfalcon dominates most birds and small mammals that inhabit the Arctic. Although fairly dependent on ptarmigan, this raptor can also overtake snow geese and elusive Arctic hares. Launching from an observation perch or diving from a soar, the gyrfalcon usually can capture its target on the first attempt. But if it misses, this persistent predator will give chase and almost always return victorious.

In the Arctic, ptarmigan, hare, and lemming populations go through cycles of abundance and scarcity. The gyrfalcon has evolved an interesting strategy to cope with the periodically erratic availability of prey. When animals are abundant, the gyrfalcon female will lay up to seven eggs. In times of scarcity, the mother will lay fewer eggs. During the winter, the species will range as far south as the windy grasslands of eastern Colorado in search of richer hunting grounds.

Gyrfalcons nest on rock islands that jut from the sea of frozen tundra, and on ledges and bluffs overlooking the broad river valleys that sweep beyond the tree line. Like other falcons, these birds do not build their own nests. They will either re-use nests made by other raptors and ravens, or they will lay eggs in a depression scraped in the debris of a rock ledge.

By the time their chicks are ten days old, gyrfalcon parents leave them unattended because both adult birds must hunt to satisfy the voracious appetites of their nestlings, and to feed themselves. While away from the nest, the adults must keep a sharp eye out for their chief nemesis, the golden eagle, which is a particularly aggressive predator of young gyrfalcons.

The gyrfalcon can appear in a variety of colors, ranging from pure white to dark gray, and every mixture of shades in between. Little was known about the bird's natural lifestyle until the mid-1900s, when Arctic explorers made the first scientific observations.

More recent studies suggest that the gyrfalcon population is stable, if not growing. Even so, sightings are uncommon because few people have the opportunity or the fortitude to see this bird in its remote natural habitat. The rest of us must wait for a particularly harsh winter, when a wayward gyrfalcon may wing its way well into the more temperate latitudes of the American West on a blast of Arctic wind.

Gyrfalcon

Falco rusticolus

(right) The gyrfalcon will often re-use a nest built on a rock ledge by another raptor or raven.

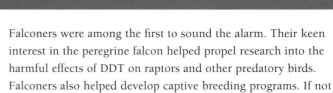

FOR NEARLY A THOUSAND YEARS, people have enjoyed a special bond with peregrine falcons. There was a time when these "noble hawks" were deemed worthy to be raised in captivity by aristocratic falconers only. And yet, today, peregrine falcons owe their continued survival in the wild to legions of conservation-minded common folk.

Pointed wings, stiff flight feathers, and special muscular and skeletal adaptations combine to make the peregrine falcon one of the fastest and strongest birds in the world. In its characteristic hunting stoop, this raptor can fall to earth in pursuit of prey at speeds of more than two hundred miles per hour.

The peregrine falcon will strike its quarry with an open foot at first, reserving the option of either grabbing on with the other foot or delivering a stunning blow, depending on the size of the prey. I once observed a wild peregrine falcon dispatch a cattle egret by first smacking it on the head and then wheeling around, grabbing the egret's back, and killing it with a bite to the neck.

Find a promontory overlooking land or sea, or a deep canyon anywhere in the American West, and you are liable to locate a peregrine falcon nest. The Grand Canyon in northern Arizona holds perhaps the greatest concentration of peregrine nesting sites outside of Alaska. Half a century ago, however, these birds were few and far between.

Populations of the peregrine falcon and many other raptor species declined precipitously in the years following World War Two, coincident with the widespread use of pesticides such as DDT.

Peregrine Falcon

Falco peregrinus

Falconers were among the first to sound the alarm. Their keen interest in the peregrine falcon helped propel research into the harmful effects of DDT on raptors and other predatory birds. Falconers also helped develop captive breeding programs. If not for the release of birds reared from healthy, captive adults, peregrine falcons would not be nearly as abundant on the east coast of the United States as they are today.

In 1999, peregrine falcon fans celebrated as the species was officially removed from the list of endangered species. Today, it is common to see peregrine falcons flying along the beaches of the Pacific during fall and spring, heading to and from wintering areas in Mexico and South America, and skimming the sand and shallows for shorebirds en route.

Some birds opt to spend the winter in coastal and Southwestern cities, and even nest on tall, man-made structures such as skyscrapers and bridges that provide ideal perches from which to hunt for pigeons and other urban birds. Others prefer life on the wild side. Wherever they roost, peregrine falcons are associating more closely with humans today than ever before, and both man and bird are healthier for the relationship.

Pointed wings, stiff flight feathers, and special muscular and skeletal adaptations combine to make the peregrine falcon one of the fastest and strongest birds in the world (left and above).

*Falcons differ from other
diurnal raptors in the manner
in which they kill.*

I N THE HALF LIGHT BEFORE DAWN on a morning in May, I awoke to the simple calls of white-winged doves, curve-billed thrashers, and cactus wrens echoing off the sheer rock wall that sheltered our desert campsite. Just as the sun peeked above the northeastern horizon, the piercing, wailing cry ol a prairie falcon brought the avian chorus to a climax.

Prairie Falcon

Falco mexicanus

Looking up, I spotted the mottled marauder, perched at the precipice of the bluff. I watched breathlessly as it scanned the desert below and then spread its slender wings and dropped straight down to take an unsuspecting small bird or mammal. Who needs a cup of coffee when one can rise to such an exhilarating sight?

Falcons differ from other diurnal raptors in the manner in which they kill. A tomial tooth on the upper mandible enables the prairie falcon to instantly severe the neck vertebrae of its victim. This tooth is absent from the beaks of hawks, which use their powerful feet and talons to grip, pierce, and crush prey.

Prairie falcons do not construct nests. Instead, they scrape out depressions in the gravel of rock potholes or well-protected cliff ledges. Occasionally, they will use abandoned, stick-built nests of

(left) A tomial tooth on the upper mandible enables the prairie falcon to instantly severe the neck vertebrae of its victim.

*Prairie falcons occur only
from southwestern Canada
to the Mexican border,
but in certain localities
they can be very abundant.*

other raptors. A typical clutch consists of about five eggs, but infertility and predation by mammals take their toll and few will hatch and survive to leave the nest. Dangerous living also claims a high percentage of fledgling prairie falcons, which have a tendency to collide with objects during high-speed chases.

This species has the most restricted range of any falcon in North America. Prairie falcons occur only from southwestern Canada to the Mexican border, but in certain localities they can be very abundant. The Snake River Birds of Prey Natural Area in Idaho was set aside as a landscape of national importance in part because of the density of prairie falcons that nest along the canyon walls and find good hunting on the high desert that rolls back from either rim. Nests tend to be located close together, and during March and April the air is filled with noisy falcons fighting over slivers of territory.

During the fall and winter months, many of the rodents that inhabit this raptor's upland breeding habitats spend more time underground and out of sight, and so the prairie falcons drift into the lowlands in search of migrating birds.

The same agricultural areas that supply Americans with much of their winter fruits and vegetables also attract the feathered quarry prairie falcons favor. During this time of the year no penetrating "song" will announce a prairie falcon's presence: That is reserved for the courting and nesting season. But you can still see them silently perching on power poles, trees, and fence posts, or soaring gracefully overhead.

The voice of the prairie falcon is only heard during the courting and nesting season (right). During the winter months, the bird remains silent (above).

THE BARN OWL IS THE ONLY nocturnal raptor in a genus all its own. One of the avian world's most adaptable predators, the barn owl occurs on all continents except Antarctica. In the Western Hemisphere, its range extends from the tip of South America to the central United States.

The barn owl usually nests in the recesses of trees and in rocky potholes. Yet, as its name implies, this species has become accustomed to making a home in barns and other man-made structures that provide shelter, security, and close proximity to prey. In the urban Southwest, they will even nest in exotic palm trees.

In most regions, barn owls live in their nesting territories year round. After leaving the nest, the fledglings disperse and may fly more than one hundred miles away from their natal homes to find territories of their own. In years when the weather is extremely bad or prey populations decline significantly, even adult barn owls will move to find more favorable conditions.

Barn Owl

Tyto alba

A barn owl female can lay up to eleven eggs at a time, and in years when prey is abundant she may begin to lay a second clutch of eggs before the first group of nestlings leaves the nest. Thus barn owls can maximize reproduction during years of abundance, which compensates for lean years.

To communicate its presence and intent in the dark of night, the barn owl has evolved a wide array of calls, from eerie screams and hisses to whistles and snores. Just about the only sound this species doesn't make is the "hoot" so commonly associated with owls.

As its name implies, the barn owl (right) will nest in barns and other man-made structures that provide shelter, security, and close proximity to prey to feed its nestlings (above).

This stealthy hunter's acute senses of hearing and night vision enable it to detect and capture small mammals that other raptors miss. The barn owl hunts on the wing, listening for the slightest sound and tipping its wings to dip down after the first thing that moves.

People and barn owls frequently occupy the same buildings. An owl's presence usually goes unnoticed until regurgitated pellets begin to pile up beneath its favorite perches. These pellets can be messy to clean up, but one also can learn a great deal about a barn owl's diet and lifestyle by studying its pellets.

One entrepreneurial scientist, Dr. Irwin Slesnick, has built a thriving business by collecting, packaging, and marketing barn owl pellets to schools. Grade-schoolers get to examine these pellets up close and are invariably fascinated by what they find.

The western screech owl
is one of the most widely
heard owls in the West.

ITS VOCAL REPERTOIRE IS UNMATCHED by any other owl in the American West, and it is as likely to be heard in the temperate rain forests of Alaska as in the warm desert scrub of New Mexico. Perhaps the most characteristic sound this owl makes is the "bouncing ball" call. If you are hiking up a canyon lined with cottonwood and sycamore trees and you hear something that sounds like a rubber ball, dropped from shoulder height and thumping the ground with increasing rapidity as its energy expires, you have heard a western screech-owl.

Adult western screech owls reside year round in the same general area in which they breed, and their fledglings usually don't stray very far once they leave the nest in autumn. These owls are habitat generalists that can survive just about anyplace, provided there are plenty of trees with nesting holes and open areas nearby with abundant small mammals, insects, and small birds on which to prey. This owl has even been known to nest in low-density residential neighborhoods.

If the western screech-owl could be said to have its own niche, it would be in canyons and riparian areas lined with deciduous trees, where the bird doesn't have to compete with other small owls like the flammulated and northern saw-whet. In prime habitat with abundant prey, western screech-owl nests may be located no farther apart than the length of a football field.

Western Screech-Owl

Otus kennicottii

The western screech-owl hunts from perches, capturing prey after a short dash to the ground. Its broad wings beat very rapidly, and it almost never hovers or glides.

Like so many other small owls of the American West, the western screech-owl relies upon cavities that woodpeckers and flickers create. In March, the male will begin to make his "bouncing ball" call to define his territory. He and his mate also will initiate, or renew, their courtship with mutual preening and synchronized duets. To demonstrate the quality of his territory and his prowess as a hunter, the male will gather prey for his mate. This display is perhaps the most important one of all, because from the beginning of courtship until the young are half grown the male essentially will act as the sole provider.

The western screech-owl readily responds to imitations or recordings of its territorial call, but the best way to experience one is to enter its domain on a moonlit night and just listen. If you should catch a glimpse of one as it swoops onto a perch, consider yourself lucky. The western screech-owl may be one of the most widely heard owls in the West, but it is still uncommon to see one in the wild.

(right) The "bouncing ball" call that the male western screech owl makes to define his territory is perhaps its most characteristic sound.

92

*A fierce predator
of just about anything
that crawls or perches,
the great horned owl is
particularly fond of rabbits.*

##

Great Horned Owl

*Bubo
virginianus*

WINGED TIGER OF THE NIGHT, the great horned owl has been an object of curiosity and superstition for centuries. This huge owl is almost two feet long from head to tail tip, and its ears add another couple inches, at least. Its call is the familiar and unmistakable Ho-ho, Hoooo, Hooo hoot. Less familiar is a screechy, drawn-out whistle that ends with an inflection. This is the sound mates and fledglings make to convey their locations to one another.

During the day, great horned owls can be difficult for birdwatchers to spot because they rely on complex camouflage coloration and a still posture to blend in amid a lair of dense branches or against the trunk of a tree.

Highly adaptable, resourceful, and ubiquitous, the great horned owl can be found in just about every habitat and climate zone in the Western Hemisphere, from the densest forest to the most barren desert. This owl is usually a permanent resident wherever it occurs, and will defend its nesting territory almost year round. Only in the northern extremes of its range, when prey becomes scarce, will this species venture far from its territory to search for food.

The great horned owl hunts exclusively at night, from a perch, and glides on drooped and silent wings to snatch its unsuspecting victim. A fierce predator of just about anything that crawls or perches, the great horned owl is particularly fond of rabbits but can adapt to whatever prey is locally available.

(right) The great horned owl can be difficult to spot because its coloration enables it to blend in amid a lair of dense branches or against the trunk of a tree.

*Nest building is not the
great horned owl's forte.*

Few other raptors, whether diurnal or nocturnal, can rest easy when the great horned owl is about. I have discovered the remains of both American kestrels and Western screech-owls in great horned owl nests, and they have been known to take many other species as well. In the 1980s, some of the first attempts to reintroduce captive-bred peregrine falcons to the wild were compromised by the presence of the great horned owl in several habitats.

The great horned owl does not shy away from human habitation, and often will nest adjacent to golf courses and other open spaces. When this predator takes up residence in suburbia, no family night-prowling cat in the neighborhood is safe.

Nest building is not the great horned owl's forte. Instead, the male will claim a nest formerly constructed by another species of raptor, most commonly the red-tailed hawk. I have checked nests on cliff faces and in tall trees that red-tailed hawks and Harris's hawks had occupied the year before, only to find great horned owls, hunkered down with ears flat against their heads, trying in vain to remain concealed.

It is not unusual, in the light of day, for local bird life on which the great horned owl preys to become emboldened at the sight of a hapless fledgling and to mob it mercilessly for the sins of its elders. But after sunset, under cover of darkness, the owl will exact its vengeance.

The adult, great horned owl (far left) that resides in the deserts of the American southwest is lighter and grayer than its forest-dwelling counter-part (preceding page), but as hatchlings (left) they look the same.

97

To avoid being eaten itself by other raptors,
this owl has a color pattern on the back of its
neck that resembles two watchful eyes.

SURVIVING YEAR ROUND in the pine-forested mountains of the American West can be a challenge for any winged predator. But for the northern pygmy owl, which is only seven inches tall and has a very high metabolic rate, the need to maintain a constant body temperature means it must hunt almost as much during the day as it does at night.

Swooping inconspicuously from perch to perch, hugging the ground and blending in with its surroundings to avoid startling prey, the northern pygmy-owl pounces on everything from small mammals and birds to insects and reptiles. To avoid being eaten itself by other raptors, this owl has a color pattern on the back of its neck that resembles two watchful eyes. The northern pygmy-owl can also fool potential predators with its call: the bird is something of a ventriloquist, and the series of soft hoots it makes can seem to originate from someplace other than where the owl actually is.

Because the northern pygmy-owl cannot afford to go for long without eating, it pursues a catch-and-cache strategy, hiding large amounts of prey in places too small for larger owls and forest hawks to raid. If the winter weather turns especially bleak, live prey becomes scarce, and the food caches run low, the northern pygmy-owl will simply move down slope in search of sustenance.

As spring arrives, the male northern pygmy-owl begins to delineate his territory with a series of one-note hoots and perform courtship displays that consist of mock pursuit-and-attack flights. In April or May, the female selects a hole in a pine or deciduous tree in which to lay a clutch of about three eggs. The northern pygmy-owl is unique among western owls in that the female won't begin to incubate her eggs until every one is laid. For about a month, the male must keep himself and his mate fed while she minds the nest. Then, within a day or two of each other, the eggs hatch. Less than four weeks later, the owlets are fully feathered, and a week after that the fledglings leave the nest.

The northern pygmy-owl is an ubiquitous inhabitant of mountain ranges and high-elevation riparian drainages throughout the West, and yet ornithologists still know surprisingly little about the species. Perhaps it's because, unlike some of its more high-profile cousins in the avian world, this raptor has seldom come in conflict with people.

This species does not appear to be threatened or endangered. Some investigations have suggested that the northern pygmy-owl might actually benefit from limited timber harvest programs, which could create the more open forest environment this owl requires. At the very least, the northern pygmy-owl merits greater study.

Northern Pygmy-Owl

Glaucidium gnoma

(right) The northern pygmy-owl has a very high metabolic rate and cannot afford to go for long without eating, so it pursues a catch-and-cache strategy.

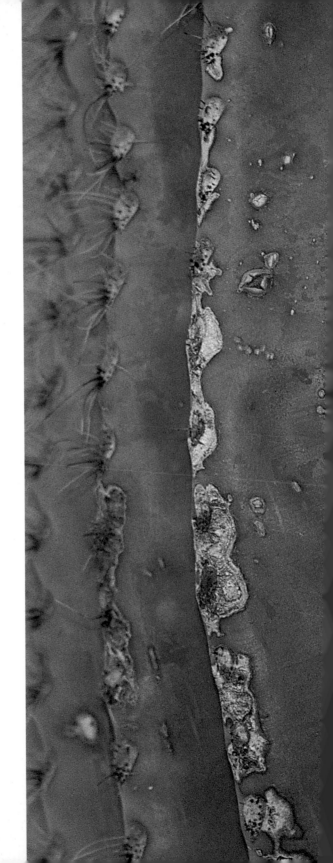

*The ferruginous pygmy owl will
forage during the day in order
to feed its hungry young later.*

TUCKED IN THE CAVITY OF A SAGUARO, yellow eyes wide open at midday, the ferruginous pygmy-owl has one thing on its mind: survival. How the human invasion of its Sonoran Desert homeland will influence this pugnacious little owl has been hotly debated ever since it was declared an endangered species in 1997.

Ferruginous Pygmy-Owl

*Glaucidium
brasilianum*

Relatively common in southern Texas, lowland areas of Mexico, and throughout the neotropics, the ferruginous pygmy-owl has significantly declined as a permanent resident in the American Southwest, which is at the northwestern extreme of its range. Historical records suggest that riverine woodlands of southern Arizona were the habitat of choice for this tiny owl. Recently, however, biologists have found about a third of Arizona's known population in upland deserts that are in the path of development. Because fledgling owlets frequently

(right) *The ferruginous pygmy owl was once fairly common in southern Arizona, but today its status as a permanent resident in this northwestern extreme of its range appears to be very tenuous.*

sit in the open, they can be easy prey for desert dwellers like Harris's hawks and great horned owls, as well as newcomers, such as neighborhood cats. Habitat that affords protective cover for adults and young is therefore essential.

The ferruginous pygmy-owl aggressively pursues small birds and mammals, lizards, and insects, and often takes prey twice its size. Although an adult stands only about six inches tall, it can kill mourning doves and large spiny lizards with a quick flight and grab that result in a victorious tussle on the ground. The ferruginous pygmy-owl is commonly mobbed by other birds, which instantly recognize it as a fierce desert predator that needs to be exposed and hassled.

Since this owl hunts frequently during the day and its feathers lack the fine structures needed to mute its flight, the ferruginous pygmy-owl relies more on speed and deception than stealth. The spots on the back of its head look like eyes and may trick prey into thinking the bird is looking in one direction when actually it is glaring in the other.

In the desert Southwest, ferruginous pygmy owl pairs commonly take over saguaro cavities excavated by woodpeckers or flickers. The female owl will lay about four eggs and incubate them for about four weeks. A month after they hatch, the owlets leave the nest. These owls are usually found in or near their nests, calling during the morning and early evening hours at the onset of breeding, and foraging commonly during the day in order to feed hungry young.

Ferruginous pygmy-owl pairs typically take over saguaro cavities excavated by woodpeckers and flickers, and their owlets (above) are ready to fledge a month after they hatch (left).

*Holes in columnar cacti
make excellent homes for
the desert-dwelling elf owl.*

O N MOONLIT NIGHTS, the smallest owl in the American West certainly can make a big racket. This incessant chatter on the part of male elf owls serves notice of their breeding intent. Elf owls usually nest in very close proximity to one another, and so the imperative for each male to defend its tiny territory is great.

Elf Owl

Micrathene
whitneyi

The elf owl breeding range is confined to the woodlands, riparian corridors, and Sonoran Desert of southern Arizona and northern Mexico. This latter, lushly vegetated habitat is dominated by dense stands of saguaros, and this is where the greatest concentrations of elf owls can be found.

Northern flickers and Gila woodpeckers are essential to elf owl ecology because they excavate nest holes in the giant columnar cacti that later serve as homes for elf owls. Inside a saguaro cavity, the temperature can be as much as sixteen degrees cooler than the air outside. Elf owls, which stand less than six inches tall, are not particular about the size or orientation of their nest holes.

The elf owl has no fear of people, and frequently takes advantage of urban landscaping. Suburban backyard gardens attract lots of insects, and if saguaros are also present elf owls will

(right) The tiny elf owl will hover to snatch flying insects and walk about to capture crawling beetles and scorpions as well.

*Elf owls stand less
than six inches tall.*

not hesitate to take up residence. That is, unless all the available holes are already occupied by non-native house sparrows or European starlings.

Elf owls typically will mate in years when the desert is carpeted with spring wildflowers, the seeds of which require sufficient winter rains in order to germinate. These flowers attract insects on which the birds feed. If winter rainfall is scant and the spring bloom is poor, the owls may not be stimulated to breed. By the time the summer rainy season begins in July, the opportunity for the owls to breed has passed.

In mid March of a good year, the elf owl breeding season begins. Males arrive first and attract mates with their varied calls. Usually, the female will lay three eggs and the male will gather enough food to feed the entire family. All sorts of insects, attracted by the spring blossoms, fill the air and scurry around the desert floor. Elf owls hover to snatch grounded prey, dart after flying insects, and walk about to capture crawling beetles and scorpions.

During the Sonoran Desert winter, nighttime temperatures frequently fall below freezing and nocturnal insect activity stops. Before the first frost, elf owls fly south to spend the winter. There, these littlest owls remain relatively silent, saving their voices for springtime.

Elf owls depend upon Northern flickers and Gila woodpeckers to excavate the holes in which they make their nests (right), and will frequently hunt for insects amid urban landscaping (left).

WHO WOULD SUSPECT that the helpless half-grown babies of a bird that stands less than ten inches tall could cause a man to recoil in terror? Yet this is exactly what happened one day a few years back when a colleague of mine tried to inspect the underground nest of a burrowing owl and was greeted by a "rattlesnake hiss" chorus from the nervous nestlings within. This astonishing ability to mimic the sound of a deadly venomous snake enables burrowing owls to frighten not just nosy researchers but predators as well. It is just one of several intriguing behavioral adaptations unique to this ground-dwelling owl.

Burrowing owls are very particular about where they choose to nest, and as a result they are relatively successful at fledging young. The name "burrowing owl" is something of a misnomer: This bird almost never excavates its own den, preferring instead to let ground squirrels, kangaroo rats, and especially prairie dogs do the digging for them.

Most burrowing owls nest in prairie dog towns. After first defining the boundaries of his breeding territory with soft *coo-coo* calls, a male burrowing owl will select an abandoned burrow within the town that will shelter his mate and brood for several

Burrowing Owl

Athene cunicularia

months. Next, the bird will gather prairie dog feces, place some around the burrow entrance, and use other pieces to line the nesting chamber. Some observers have suggested that burrowing owls use this material to mask their own odor and thus deter predators.

Burrowing owl nesting sites tend to be located on grasslands and open desert areas where the ground is relatively flat and porous and there is scattered low vegetation. Nests have even been found on golf courses and at airports. The birds watch for potential predators and prey by perching on elevated rodent mounds as well as fence posts, windmills, and other man-made structures.

The burrowing owl is an aggressive bird that usually preys on insects and small mammals, such as mice and voles, but can tackle fare as large as a full-grown dove. This owl is also clever and resourceful: One summer night in the parking lot of a convenience store, I watched a burrowing owl feast on beetles as they rained down from a streetlight. While these owls usually hunt at night, during the breeding season it is not uncommon to find one out and about at midday, looking for a meal.

During the nineteenth century, burrowing owl populations declined throughout the West as farmers eliminated the towns of burrowing mammals like prairie dogs. In the twentieth century, a new conservation ethic emerged and scores of grassland reserves were established in which niche species, including the burrowing owl, could survive and thrive. These extraordinary creatures have proven to be a big draw, and are helping to "sell" the public on the value of saving these special habitats.

(right and above) Burrowing owls tend to nest on grasslands and open desert where the ground is relatively flat and porous and there is scattered low vegetation.

*These secretive owls drop silently
onto unsuspecting prey from
hidden canopy perches.*

IMMENSE CONIFERS—as old as the nation itself—form a
soaring, sheltering canopy, penetrated only occasionally by
shafts of sunlight. Here in nature's cathedral, a heavenly incense
of pine and fir boughs permeates the moist, cool air. This is the
fragile domain of the spotted owl.

Since the 1990s, when the U.S Fish and Wildlife Service first
listed the spotted owl as a threatened species, it has been at the
center of great debate about the stewardship of old-growth forests
in the American West. These forests afford ecologically unique
habitat for the spotted owl, as well as economically valuable timber.
How much habitat is required to support a sustainable spotted owl
population, and which remaining tracts of old-
growth forest must be preserved, undisturbed,
to maintain species viability? These remain issues
of great interest and concern both to conservationists and to those who rely on the forest for their
livelihood.

Mature forests, dominated by tall trees that
are more than two hundred years old, provide
the specific habitat the spotted owl requires. The
Mexican spotted owl, a subspecies found in the
Southwest, inhabits shaded, rocky canyons that have a damp and
chilly ambience similar to that of old growth forests in the Pacific
Northwest. Spotted owls select these environs because, unlike the
ubiquitous great horned owl, they are less able to regulate their
body temperature through panting.

The spotted owl feeds mainly on small mammals. In the
Pacific Northwest, the flying squirrel is an important food source.
In the Southwest, wood rats are the favored fare. The diet of the

*Spotted
Owl*

*Strix
occidentalis*

Mexican spotted owl is more variable, and includes lizards, bats,
and insects. These secretive owls drop silently onto unsuspecting
prey from hidden canopy perches. They hunt mostly at night, but
will leave a secluded day roost to capture quarry if the opportunity
presents itself.

Whole and uneaten portions of prey are often cached on a
limb near the roost or nest. Joe Ganey, an authority on the
Mexican spotted owl, once watched helplessly as roosting owls
flew over to retrieve their cache when they realized
Joe was about to claim the food for scientific
scrutiny. As this experience suggests, and other
research confirms, spotted owls have no particular
fear of humans.

Spotted owls do not breed every year. Instead,
they follow cycles of prey abundance and scarcity,
nesting when conditions for feeding owlets are
most favorable. They use tree cavities, old nests
built by other raptors, or any flat and protected
structure in the snarled branches of large, mature trees.

It was once thought that spotted owls were entirely sedentary,
but more recent studies have shown that this is not true. They
may, in fact, depart from their immediate breeding area, but will
not venture beyond the bounds of the old growth forest. Without
question, therefore, the fate of the spotted owl is inextricably
linked to these epic trees.

*(right) The Mexican spotted owl, a Southwestern subspecies, inhabits
shaded canyons that have a damp, chilly ambience similar to that of old
growth forests.*

*In most parts of the Southwest, long-eared owls
are somewhat nomadic breeders, nesting during
years when prey is especially abundant.*

STRUGGLING IN THE DARK through a tamarisk thicket, sweat dripping off our faces, we were so preoccupied watching for rattlesnakes lurking in the underbrush that we almost didn't hear it. The sound, faint at first, was like someone blowing on the end of a Coke bottle. Was someone signaling us?

Suddenly, a flutter of wings, and up ahead the nest of a long-eared owl came alive in the beam of our flashlight. Mother owl, no less startled than we, swooshed into the dark to join her calling mate.

This handsome owl, with its reddish facial disk and orange colored eyes, can be found throughout the temperate regions of the Northern Hemisphere. In most parts of the Southwest, long-eared owls are somewhat nomadic breeders, nesting during years when prey is especially abundant. Elsewhere, they are sedentary and permanently occupy areas near nesting sites. Some populations are so densely distributed during the breeding season that they can be considered loosely colonial.

The long-eared owl can nest in a variety of habitats. I have spotted pairs in a nest once occupied by a northern goshawk in a Ponderosa pine, an abandoned Cooper's hawk nest in a hackberry tree along a woodland riparian corridor, and an old Harris's hawk nest in a Sonoran Desert saguaro cactus. In the arid Southwest, long-eared owls that occupy a particular nest one season often will not be found there the following year, and may not even return to the vicinity.

Long-eared owls are nocturnal hunters except in the northern extremes of their range, where short nights and hungry nestlings

Long-eared Owl

Asio otus

compel parents to forage in daylight. They eat mammals, usually small ones like mice and voles, and will tend to specialize on only one or two species of prey, depending on location. In Arizona, for example, kangaroo rats are a favorite item.

During the cold winter months, long-eared owls can be found in areas where prey is plentiful, and they will associate in roosts of as many as fifty birds. These owls generally roost in trees, and will tend to perch higher in warm weather and lower during cold snaps. In areas where owls are permanent residents, these communal roosts form the focal point from which breeding pairs disperse in spring to nest nearby. During the nesting season, long-eared owls will continue to rely on the same sources of prey that sustained them through the winter.

When discovered during the daytime, the long-eared owl stands tall and still, with its wings tight against its body as though trying to appear two-dimensional. The ears for which this owl is named become erect, the signal that it is about to fly away. Consider those long ears your cue to back up slowly and let the owl rest.

After dark, when this species is more likely to be out and about, it's worth a trip back to the roost to see what revelations exist in the pellets beneath the perches. There, with flashlight in hand, you too may have an up-close encounter with the flapping wings of a long-eared owl.

(left) When discovered during the daytime, the long-eared owl stands tall and still, with its wings tight against its body and its ears erect.

EARLY AMERICAN PIONEERS, who often found themselves alone in the wilderness, learned to listen carefully for sounds both familiar and strange. Was that metallic, rasping noise coming from a sawmill in a settlement around the bend? Or could it be something else entirely—perhaps a warning from a different sort of "woodsman" perched nearby? When these English-speaking settlers discovered a little owl whose alarm call sounded remarkably like a whetstone striking a saw blade, it seemed only natural to call this bird the northern saw-whet owl. The name sounds unusual to us today, but it made a lot of sense to folks back then.

As one of the most migratory of the small, mammal-eating owls, the northern saw-whet owl is most likely to be encountered in transit. Its diet consists mainly of mice, shrews, and voles, but this aggressive, eight-inch predator has been known to take mammals as big as flying squirrels and birds the size of the northern cardinal as well. The northern saw-whet owl generally chooses a low perch from which to spot and pounce on prey. With long wings relative to its light body, the bird is well equipped to outmaneuver its quarry.

The most commonly heard vocalization the northern saw-whet owl makes is a series of single-noted whooping calls, one or two seconds apart. During the spring mating season, the male may whoop it up, nonstop, for hours as it proclaims its territory.

A common nester in spruce-fir forests throughout the West, the northern saw-whet owl also will nest in mixed deciduous

Northern Saw-whet Owl

Aegolius acadicus

forests along mountain streams. It avoids vast expanses of pines, preferring to make its home in a patchwork of pine and deciduous trees with a well-developed understory of brush and grass. A nesting pair will take over an abandoned woodpecker cavity, and in April or May the female will lay up to seven eggs. The young take wing in about five weeks, and by September all northern saw-whet owls begin to migrate south from their breeding areas.

The northern saw-whet owl is closely related to its larger cousin, the boreal owl, which occurs farther north in North America and only moves south during winters when prey in its traditional habitat become scarce. Why the northern saw-whet should be so highly migratory, while the boreal owl is not, is a mystery.

During the winter months, the northern saw-whet owl takes up residence in relatively open areas that do not resemble its breeding habitat of mixed conifer and deciduous, riparian forests. Here, the noisy little bird of spring and summer becomes silent because it no longer needs to defend its territory or sound the alarm. Experienced birders will need to look very carefully to find this little owl with the unusually large head and tuft-less ears, because the northern saw-whet is unlikely to reveal its presence by taking to the air abruptly or uttering its call.

(right) The northern saw-whet owl is named for its alarm call, which sounds remarkably like a "saw-whet" stone striking a blade.

Acknowledgments

VARIOUS PEOPLE ARE ESPECIALLY RESPONSIBLE for my knowledge of, and appreciation for, western raptors. Their actions continue to remind me of the power and influence of one's deeds and words, however seemingly small and insignificant at the time. They have added wonder and abundance to my life.

For sharing their passion for raptor conservation around campfires in canyons or over a drink at a meeting, or for expressing their thrill for raptors during trips afield, I wish to acknowledge Skip Ambrose, Bud Anderson, Brent Bibles, Erick Campbell, Rick Erman, Grainger Hunt, Lloyd Kiff, Mike Kochert, Lee Kohlhase, G. Donald Kucera, Seymour and Jim Levy, Ray Logan, Bill Mannan, Brian Millsap, Don Prentice, Richard Sloan, Virgil Weitzel, and Clayton White.

Finally, I am grateful to Tom Vezo, who has added an awesome dimension to my view of raptors through his photography.

— RICHARD L. GLINSKI

Photographer's Notes

THE PHOTOS IN THIS BOOK WERE TAKEN EXCLUSIVELY with a 35mm Nikon F5 camera body and various Nikon lenses, including a 600mm f4 AFS ED Nikkor DII and a AFS Nikkor 300mm f2.8 DII, both with and without the TC-14E-II 1.4X tele-converter. Other lenses used were the 80-200mm f2.8 IF-ED zoom, 200mm f4-D AF micro lens, and 24-120mm f3.5-5.6 D zoom. For stability, I used a Gitzo 1549 carbon fiber tripod with a Foba Superball tripod head.

I chose to use Fujichrome Velvia for most of the portraits, and Fujichrome Provia F 100 pushed to 200 ISO for many of the action shots, especially the raptors in flight.

— TOM VEZO

I'D LIKE TO ACKNOWLEDGE the following people for their help, support, and friendship throughout my adventures on this project. First and foremost, publisher Ross Humphreys accompanied me in the field and, through his contacts, enabled me to photograph in some difficult areas. My editor, Ronald J. Foreman, came up with the idea for this book, and I thank him for having faith in my photography and challenging me to take on this assignment. I also am grateful to Rich Glinski, who taught me so much about raptors and helped me locate some of the more hard-to-find species. I would like to thank Larry Lindahl for his exceptional design ideas and keen eye for photography. He put in an extraordinary amount of time and effort that resulted in an outstanding book design.

I wouldn't have had the freedom to spend as much time on the road and in the field without the able assistance of Moira McMahon, my office manager. Along the way, I also received invaluable help from Alison D'Amato, Peter and Gerlind H. Bartels, Rick Bowers, Mike Danzenbaker, Chuck Graham, John Harris, Ned Harris, Phil and Karren Hunke, Jerry and Vera Iser, Kevin Karlson, Kenn Kaufman, Jean Keene, Ken McVay, John Mullin, Carol and Jack Murray, Glenn Proudfoot, Ben Schwartz, Kai Simonsen, Helen and Noel Snyder, Dorothy Vezo, Dr. Richard Wagner, and Paul Zimmerman.

David and Lisle Collister at Santa Rita Lodge and Luis Calvo, Nancy Hertel, and Jenni Tobias at Chuparosa Inn extended their gracious hospitality.

Finally, I could not have completed the photography for this book without the help of Scott Richardson, Dennis Abatte, and Shawn Lowrey at the Arizona Game and Fish Department; Bronwyn Davey and Marlon Concepción at the California Condor Recovery Program; and Dave Gardner, Joyce Gerrits, and Jim Crawley at Nikon Inc.

— TOM VEZO

Elf owl (left) and bald eagle (following page)